PANORAMA OF WORLD ART

———

PREHISTORIC
EUROPEAN ART

PREHISTORIC

EUROPEAN ART

Text by WALTER TORBRÜGGE

HARRY N. ABRAMS, INC. Publishers NEW YORK

End papers:

Stags (or *Reindeer*) *Crossing a Stream with Fish,* impression rolled from an engraved staff. Reindeer antler, length 9³/₄″. From Lortet (Hautes-Pyrénées), France. Musée des Antiquités Nationales, Saint-Germain-en-Laye

Translated from the German by Norbert Guterman

Library of Congress Catalog Card Number: 68-28390

Contents

Introduction

PREFATORY NOTE. Only a small portion of the Prehistoric artifacts that have come down to us can be classified as strictly artistic; however, it is impossible to grasp the significance of any of them without reference to their cultural background. As it is, a great deal still remains problematical or unknown. Since a general introduction to Prehistory would be out of place here, each section is followed by a map of the sites and a chronological chart of the period with which it deals. The maps are intended merely to indicate the find spots of the objects illustrated in this book and do not cover all the existing sites. As for the chronological charts, the simplest possible indications have been given, precise dating being in many cases still a matter of scholarly controversy. The tables on pages 253–54 give an over-all view of the entire period.

The book is divided chronologically according to the main cultural periods, and within each of these divisions similar kinds of product are grouped together. Naturally, the periods are not equal in artistic or cultural importance, nor were all types of artifact produced in every age. Now and again, the strict archaeological sequence has been abandoned in order to follow the development of particular styles or motifs. This applies especially to the period covering the Bronze Age and the Early Iron Age, which otherwise breaks down into a multiplicity of geographical and chronological subdivisions.

PERIOD AND ENVIRONMENT. Any evaluation of Prehistoric art is necessarily bound up with the conditions that gave rise to it. Aesthetic effects rarely seem to be deliberate, although such an intention can never be entirely ruled out. Again and again, we are dealing with primitive modes of expression and figuration in which man's relationship to his environment plays the crucial part. The formal expression of perceived reality reflects a specific stage of artistic awareness that is very different from that resulting from intellectual reflection. At both stages, the work of art must primarily be seen in terms of its time and place of origin. Furthermore, figural representation and ornamentation are frequently associated with magical practices, and these in turn reflect varying stages of cultural development.

The range of artifacts produced by a particular social group is limited by its technical capacities and by the prevailing economic forms. Neighboring societies, especially if they have attained a higher stage of development, can be of enormous influence. Because Prehistoric peoples were scattered over wide areas, the degree to which they influenced one another varied considerably, and this is why any over-all picture of Prehistoric material culture requires so many qualifications. For instance, the persistence of Paleolithic and Mesolithic styles in northern Europe is accounted for by conditions peculiar to the North—its remoteness from the higher Mediterranean civilizations, for instance.

We cannot, therefore, speak of any Prehistoric cultural unity, for even in the earliest periods a variety of forms coexisted. At the same time, the Prehistoric areas of Europe are clearly differentiated from the advanced civilizations of the Near East and later, particularly, of the Aegean. This is true not only of the material aspects, but also of ways of thought and life—indispensable elements in the development of art. From at least the Neolithic period on, man's conscious evolution was continually being stimulated or interrupted by outside influences. Just how the more sophisticated foreign models were transposed into the Prehistoric idiom can be illustrated in this book only by a few typical examples.

6

FROM THE PALEOLITHIC TO THE NEOLITHIC. All known Paleolithic art was produced during the latest phase of the Old Stone Age (see page 51). By this time, Neanderthal man and related human types had long been supplanted by *Homo sapiens*, who perceived in art a new means of taming the forces of nature quite as important as the discovery of fire and the invention of tools and weapons. At first, man thought of his pictorial representations as aids in controlling his environment and influencing the course of events. The representation of animals does not necessarily presuppose some kind of hunting magic, and the surviving paintings provide little evidence one way or the other on this score. However, the way in which the animal and human representations are distributed about the caves often suggests a definite plan, certain motifs occurring regularly in specific parts of the cave. Furthermore, the nature of the sites suggests that many of them must have served as places of worship, the paintings, reliefs, and drawings in them fulfilling certain prescribed functions (see page 37).

Whatever their purpose, the earliest pictorial representations were part and parcel of the visual experience of a hunting people. There is no evidence that this was a productive society in the economic sense; most of the tools, even, involved no more than the adaptation of natural objects, particularly the chipping of stones to obtain cutting edges. The naturalism of the cave paintings probably reflects this stage of development. There does not seem to have been any earlier type of treatment, which indicates that realism (in the sense of reproducing what has actually been observed) was practiced from the moment that man first discovered the ability to draw. Not until a later stage, when man began to reflect upon himself and the world around him, did he go beyond the surface of things and begin to give form to ideas.

The transition from what might be called a "physioplastic" to an "ideoplastic" conception—from the purely intuitive image to the depiction of general ideas—was gradual. On the engraved staff from Lortet (pages 30–31), fish (indicating a stream) are added to the naturalistic depiction of stags. These fish also reproduce observed reality, but a reality that reflects a higher stage of consciousness involving intellectual processes: the artist had obviously not actually seen the stags and the fish together. During the postglacial period, the naturalistic image became schematized to the point of pure formula, as in the Mesolithic rock paintings of eastern Spain (cf. page 49). Small sculptures underwent a similar evolution; the simplified realism of the female figure, for instance (cf. pages 15–19), gave way to a stylization that emphasized a few essential features only (cf. page 26). Both types of treatment go back to a prerational, magical way of thinking that was already visible in an exaggerated stress on certain parts of the body in the earlier statuettes. Thus, painting and sculpture were primarily conceived in terms of practical use, any aesthetic effect discernible being purely incidental. This is especially clear in the naturalistic animal figures skillfully adapted to the shape of implements (cf. pages 22, 33, 35). How some of these earliest features lasted as late as the Neolithic in Scandinavia is impressively illustrated by the stone club in the shape of an elk's head from Alunda (page 52). Elsewhere in Europe, Neolithic peoples had mostly taken to cultivation and were already borrowing motifs from the more advanced Mediterranean civilizations. They were also acquiring, during the Neolithic period, basic economic and technical innovations from the same sources. Animal husbandry and agriculture are productive modes of economic activity which involve a higher degree of social organization and which thus give rise to a very different attitude to the world from that of hunters and gatherers. In this connection, the decrease in naturalistic representations of wild game is less significant than the new approach to all pictorial representation—almost invariably in the direction of stylization and schematization.

Clay statuettes of women no doubt served the same magical purposes in the Neolithic period as in the Paleolithic: to promote fertility. But the new foreign models which now became more accessible were imitated only when they could be adapted to an existing schema. This is true, for example, of pre-Cycladic marble figurines, which may be regarded as talismans of motherhood (fig. 1). Like these, the upper legs of Central European statuettes are sometimes heavily emphasized, and the faces merely suggested (see page 58). Many details in the models are slavishly copied, for example, the round head, the hairdress indicated by a few lines, the disproportionately long neck, and the arms held out straight on either side (see page 59). All these features are also present in Cypriote stone statuettes (fig. 2). Here, the rendering of the hairdress and the horizontal grooves on the neck suggesting some object of personal adornment are the only concessions to realism.

Throughout the Neolithic, unarticulated clay reliefs of human figures tend toward the creation of a symbolic language (see page 61). This tendency can be even better observed in megalithic statues. In southern France, menhir statues sometimes show the entire figure, but never in the round (as their Near Eastern prototypes probably did). The figures are in relief, but always remain very much a part of the block of stone on which they are carved (see page 84). In the next stage, the figure is reduced to a geometrically schematized face (see page 83), and finally it is broken up entirely into ornamentation (see page 85) or abbreviated to a ritual sign with barely discernible nose and eyes (cf. page 139, bottom). This lengthy development is not purely automatic. Rather, it reflects an irresistible process of stylization—conscious or unconscious—which is inherent in the Prehistoric concept of representation: as thought processes become more intellectual, the depiction of objects demands the employment of abstract formulas. The simple agreement of form with prosaic reality no longer suffices to express the inner meaning of things.

◀ 1. Neolithic figurine. Marble. From the Cyclades. Private collection. After *Time,* June 18, 1965, 48

2. Neolithic figurine. Light-green steatite, height $5^1/_8''$. From Cyprus. Cyprus Museum, Nicosia. After *Schätze aus Zypern,* exhibition catalogue, Stadtmuseum, Munich, 1968, 39, no. 8 ▶

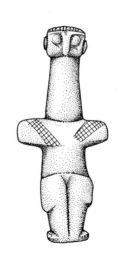

THE METAL AGE. The development away from naturalism is even more strongly marked in the Metal Age, when more and more motifs were taken from the Mediterranean civilizations. In this period, totally different artistic principles are sometimes apparent in one and the same work. Thus, the relieflike treatment of the upper body in the stele from Hirschlanden (page 135) derives from the schematic images of the dead on pole sculptures and flat stone reliefs (cf. page 134), whereas the legs were probably executed after Etruscan models. But this realistic, fully plastic treatment did not last. In the La Tène period, large sculptures once again took the form of columns or pillars (see pages 238–40). It is true that other standards prevailed in small sculptures, but this was partly for technical reasons. However, statuettes from the north of Europe in the Late Bronze Age were once again imitations of Mediterranean models. The closest counterparts of the female figures with oval faces (page 138, right), frequently with large earrings (page 137), are to be found in Etruria (fig. 3). In the North, however, they were often adapted to the shape of some implement and highly stylized, especially on the ornamented handles of razors that were probably used for ritual purposes (page 137, cf. also page 127).

While the Bronze Age proper avoided naturalism, the Urn Field period preferred schematized symbolic representations such as the stylized figures of horses and the boat with bird and sun (see pages 95, 113) Not until the Hallstatt period was the taboo against the realistic representation of man and animals lifted. This rule was, however, broken in regions north of the "cultural fault" which had direct contacts with the Mediterranean world. The story-in-pictures in the stone burial chamber at Kivik, for instance, was engraved early in the Bronze Age, and both thematically and formally it follows a Mediterranean model that could only have been brought to Scandinavia by early seafarers. It depicts a funeral ceremony, the basic elements of which are identical to a similar event painted on a sarcophagus from Hagia Triada in Crete. The similarity of certain details is truly astonishing: for instance, the combination of slender pyramids with ritual clubs (figs. 4, 5). There is probably also some connection between this scene and the gold objects from Schifferstadt, where two bronze clubs were discovered along with the conical headpiece shown on page 92.

At Kivik, the Cretan example gave rise to a peculiar blend of Nordic and Mediterranean modes of depiction. Among other things, the horses drawing the chariot are shown in profile view, in the Aegean manner (see page 132), as they are in the battle scene on a tombstone from Mycenae (page 123).

By contrast, the two wheels of the chariot are depicted schematically in the characteristic Prehistoric manner. The essential elements of an object are brought together without concern for pictorial coherence, and this is why the wheels and harness gear are not shown as they actually appear, but as individual parts of a complex structure (see page 122, top). The same principle also governs most Hallstatt or Late Bronze Age representations of men on horseback (see pages 116, 180), despite the fact that they are seen in side view. The riders seem to be standing on the backs of the horses, since the individual elements of the picture—man, horse, and reins—are only superficially combined.

Late variants of such schematic representation occur in Iberian vase painting, where the mounted man is invariably represented full length with both legs on the same side of the horse (see page 173). The Early La Tène period in Central Europe followed the same schema (fig. 6), whereas on the northern boundary of the Mediterranean world, horsemen were represented naturalistically toward the close of the Hallstatt epoch. Examples are found on the bronze situlae (deep vessels of truncated conical shape) from the region between Venice and the Alps (see pages 143, 181). Although such comparisons are dangerous, we

3. Etruscan pendant figurine. Bronze, height 2¹/₂″. From Poggio Gallinari, Italy. Museo Civico, Florence. After F. A. van Scheltema, 1950, 91, fig. 27 a

might mention here a drawing by a four-year-old child (fig. 7). At about this age, the individual attains a stage of awareness that is expressed in pictures by intellectual composition. Without any artistic training, the child has drawn a man on horseback in basically the same manner as the Prehistoric artist.

◀ 4. The lost slab from the entrance of the Bronze Age cist grave at Kivik, Skåne, Sweden (cf. pages 132–33). Height c. 47″. After L. V. Grinsell, 1942, pl. 1

5. Detail of a painted sarcophagus. Middle ▶ Minoan III, c. sixteenth century B.C. From Hagia Triada, Crete. After F. Matz, *Kreta, Mykene, Troja: Die minoische und die homerische Welt*, Stuttgart, 1956, pl. 47

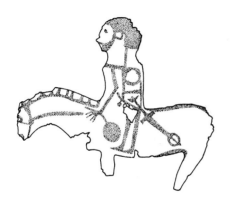

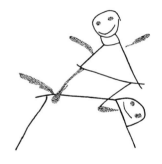

6. *Horse and Rider*. Sheet bronze, length $1^7/_8''$. From an Early La Tène wagon burial at Kärlich, Coblenz, Germany. Rheinisches Landesmuseum, Bonn. After J. Driehaus, 1965, 65, fig. 7

7. *Horse and Rider*. Drawing by Corinna ▶ Ulbert, aged four and one-half years. Starnberg, 1967

The Hallstatt artist had, of course, been exposed to Mediterranean models, and might therefore be said to have had some such training. Unquestionably, the horse statuettes from Zainingen (page 114) are copies of figures that decorated Greek pottery in the eighth century B.C. (fig. 8). But the horse and its rider from Speikern (page 177) show that artists soon fell back again into simplification and schematism; not even in sculpture could they show the horseman in the right posture. This ought not to surprise us, for even the skillful Cypriote artists were slow to master the new motif; in their early attempts, too, the rider seems to be standing on the back of his mount (fig. 9).

In drawing, the Greek treatment of the human figure was adopted only in so far as the outlines could be reduced to a geometric pattern and assimilated to the usual Hallstatt ornamentation (fig. 10). In this respect, the Mediterranean geometric styles met Prehistoric tastes more than halfway. The bodies made up of triangles and limbs constructed of straight lines are only indirectly related to the human figures on eighth-century Greek vase painting (fig. 11), but that there was some connection is unmistakable. This is confirmed by finds from southeastern Europe which supply the missing links. The same is true of the linear human figures on the

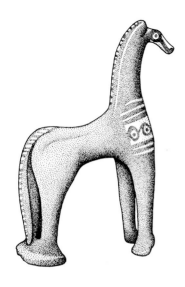

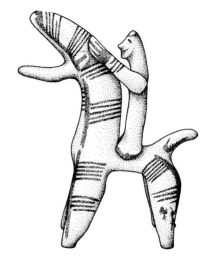

◀ 8. *Horse,* from the cover of a Geometric bowl. Terra cotta. Eighth century B.C. From Greece. Staatliche Antikensammlung. Munich. After a postcard

9. *Horse and Rider*. Terra cotta. Seventh ▶ century B.C. From Cyprus. Cyprus Museum, Nicosia. After a postcard

clay pot from Fischbach (page 116). They are lined up just like the figures in the Attic burial scene, their arms raised in mourning and both feet pointing in the same direction.

Such motifs cannot always be traced back to known models or assigned to a definite period. Especially during the La Tène epoch, certain older forms of representation more than held their own, though modified by various kinds of stylization. The gold neck ring and bracelet from Reinheim (pages 208, 209) and the fibula with masklike human faces from Parsberg (page 193) are exquisite specimens of small sculpture in which the figures are imaginatively incorporated into the ornament and adapted to the form of the object. However, the heads of birds and lions on the former and the fantastic animals on the latter are imitations of figural ornamentation on Etruscan or Greek imports of the Late Hallstatt period. As late as the fifth century B.C., in the frieze of figures on the lentiform bottle from Matzhausen (page 207), we find a hare-and-wolf motif that goes back to seventh-century Rhodian and Corinthian jugs (fig. 12).

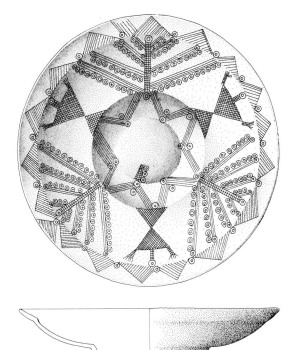

La Tène drawing, however, is ornamental in character—what the Celtic craftsman could not transform into formal ornament, he schematized. The palmettes, tendril patterns, and volutes were borrowings from the Mediterranean store of formal invention, but transformed and worked into new combinations. The proportions of Antiquity were not adhered to, perhaps were not even properly understood, as is shown by the gold-foil appliqués on the Attic bowl from Kleinaspergle (page 198). Even in masterpieces which come close to the Greek (in this case, sculptural) model, like the *Lady of Elche* in Spain, the clear classical lines of the face are overwhelmed by the mass of ornamental finery (see page 171). However, while radically transforming Mediterranean models, the strength of Celtic art lay in its very independence. It was to reach its culmination in highly abstract ornamentation (see page 222) and in large sculptures in which schematization was carried to the utmost (see page 247).

10. Bowl, stepped in cross section, with geometric ornamentation on the interior. Three schematic human figures composed of triangles, groups of straight lines, and circular impressions have been adapted to the pattern. Terra cotta, diameter 12 5/8″. Hallstatt period. From Dietldorf, Burglengenfeld, Bavaria, Germany. Museum für Vor- und Frühgeschichte, Berlin

But this was as far as it could go: Celtic art never really left the cultural climate of Prehistory. Only on the isolated far-western fringe of Europe could Celtic stylistic forms survive almost unchanged down to the Middle Ages (see page 249).

SUMMARY. In touching upon a few essential features of Prehistoric art, the emphasis has been placed on pictorial representation. This seems to cast more light on Prehistoric modes of thought and behavior than any other

11. Detail of painting on a Geometric crater from an Attic workshop, showing the funeral lamentation for a dead man on his bier. Eighth century B.C. National Museum, Athens. Simplified after P. Devambez, *Malerei im Altertum I: Griechenland und Kreta,* Gütersloh, 1963, pl. 32

aspect—precisely because it is to a high degree impersonal. What is characteristic is the way in which a given pictorial theme takes on the quality of a symbol or formula. Aesthetic elements most often play a subordinate part or are altogether absent. Needless to say, the Paleolithic and Mesolithic periods are not to be evaluated by the same criteria as the later ages in which Mediterranean influences over and over again touched off new developments. The environment is of crucial importance in two respects: first, the given stage of cultural development determines the degree of intellectual awareness in each period; and second, the nature of each group's relations with its neighbors determines to what extent it continues to develop independently or grows dependent on outside influences. Specific forms of art—especially sculpture—invariably reflect religious beliefs, types of worship, and burial customs. One leading feature of Prehistoric art is its tendency always to turn away from the naturalistic model toward abstraction.

12. Detail of painting on a Corinthian jug. Seventh century B.C. Staatliche Antikensammlung, Munich. After D. Ohly, *Die Antikensammlungen am Königsplatz in München,* n. d., pl. 6

The earliest expressions of art never rose above their inherent limitations. We are still perfectly justified in regarding the history of art proper as covered by the traditional breakdown into ancient, medieval, modern. Ancient Near Eastern, Greco-Roman, and Western art survive as categories in their own right, which cannot be thought of as "succeeding" one another. Just as no part of the ancient Mediterranean world developed wholly on its own, nor was the art of western and northern Europe shaped solely, or even primarily, by its own Prehistory. Though we cannot do without purely chronological terms like "Prehistory," "Middle Ages," and "modern times," these are not necessarily relevant to art history. Chronologically, Europe's Prehistory ended in all but a few regions with the first centuries of the Christian era. Just as Greek civilization only reached its highest development through contacts with the East, so was the meeting of the Prehistoric with the Hellenistic and Early Christian cultures the essential stimulus that gave birth to the Middle Ages in Europe.

Head of a Woman, fragment of a statuette. Ivory, height $1^1/_4''$. From the Grotte du Pape, Brassempouy (Landes), France. Musée des Antiquités Nationales, Saint-Germain-en-Laye. (See also enlargement on page 13)

Rather than ascribe the peculiar beauty of the earliest known sculptures to some "sublime accident" (Ortega y Gasset), it is far more plausible to view it as the result of a natural development. Paleolithic art—especially in its representations of man and animal—did not begin with formal experimentation. It was a reflection of reality and intended to serve a specific purpose, namely, to influence the course of things. This is precisely what accounts for the magnificent realism of the earliest known visual art, which made its appearance (roughly) in the fourth and last glacial epoch. As man became aware of the world and its manifestations, he tried to find ways of controlling nature, or at least of prevailing over it. Hard pressed by everyday reality, he was not in a position to invent abstract signs and symbols for this purpose. At least at the start, he clung to the world as he saw it. The fact that some sculptures, drawings, and paintings representing this world attained the rank of what we call art was certainly not the result of conscious purpose on the part of their makers. No early visual art was governed by aesthetic principles as we understand them. Men still lived in widely scattered groups engaged in hunting and food gathering, and appropriated the products of nature without being themselves productive in the economic

Head of a Woman, fragment of a statuette. Ivory, height c. $2''$. From Dolní Věstonice, Mikulov, Moravia, Czechoslovakia. Moravian Museum, Brno

sense. The material possessions which have come down to us comprise mainly stone and bone implements. Despite this limited selection, the tools and weapons point to a variety of differentiated activities, including specialized techniques of the hunt. This very specialization, however, implies increased dependence upon nature, not increased control over it. Therefore, the representation of the male figure plays a leading role only in cave painting, where, as a hunter, he appears in his own sphere of action. The female figure, on the other hand, predominates in small sculpture, in her opposing role as the primary element in assuring the continuity of the species and of the group. The female image became a magical invocation of fertility, the race's *sine qua non* of survival. This visual concept was consistently widespread among all Paleolithic groups, testified to in France, as in Bohemia, by finds of heads of ivory figurines. What might appear as the severe stylization of early attempts at portraiture is actually nothing but a simplification, a symbol evocative of the entire female figure. The ample forms of the *Venus of Věstonice* and other female figurines which have survived intact unequivocally reveal that these were intended to be images of motherhood.

Venus of Věstonice. Baked clay, height 4^1/$_2$″. From Dolní Věstonice, Mikulov, Moravia, Czechoslovakia. Moravian Museum, Brno

Since the female image was the embodiment of the sex rather than of a specific woman, certain essential features were exaggerated. Breasts, hips, and pudenda are invariably emphasized. Arms and legs are rarely in proportion to the rest of the body and are executed with much less care. The face is usually just a smooth surface, but hair or head ornamentation is often executed in some detail (cf. pages 13, 19). On the low relief from Laussel showing a woman holding a horn, little more is indicated than that she has long hair. The horn in her right hand has been variously interpreted. Any attempt to identify her with a Mistress of the Beasts or as the player of a propitious role in the hunt would be reaching ahead to later myths: that imaginary beings were personified and represented as human as early as the Paleolithic era is unlikely. On the other hand, the Laussel shelter, situated under a rock overhang, is a highly interesting site; it was probably a place of worship, for five stone blocks with low reliefs of human figures, mainly heavy-bodied women, were found there. Yet an indication that there is more to Paleolithic sculpture than first strikes the eye is provided by a limestone sculpture from Mauern. In the view reproduced here, we are obviously dealing with a stylized female figure with strongly emphasized buttocks. Like the *Dame de Sireuil* (page 18), the sculpture is representative of a West European type. Drawings representing similar figures have been found in the area between southern France and Bavaria, and similarly schematized figurines no more than half a finger long occur from Württemberg to Thuringia and Moravia. Looked at from another angle, however, the find from Mauern seems no less

◀ *Venus of Laussel.* Low relief on limestone, height 18¹/₂″. From the Laussel shelter, Marquay (Dordogne), France. Musée des Antiquités Nationales, Saint-Germain-en-Laye

Anthropomorphic statuette. Limestone colored with red chalk, height 2⁷/₈″. From Mauern, Neuburg an der Donau, Bavaria, Germany. Prähistorische Staatssammlung, Munich

obviously to represent a phallus and scrotum. If the work was, indeed, intended so to combine two motifs in a single object, like a puzzle picture, then it supplies evidence that the purpose of most early art was magical. This small sculpture would fall among the group of representations made in a ritual spirit to increase human and animal fertility. Its artistic or pseudoartistic effect would in this case have to be regarded as a secondary manifestation at best, even if its maker had no more in mind than the production of a schematized female statuette. The important thing is not to mistake the resemblance io a puzzle picture—the ambiguity—for some purely formal device, let alone a refinement. The strangeness is better accounted for as reflecting the peculiar bipolarity of primitive modes of thought, ever prone to find similarities in seeming opposites and to represent them as identical.

As might be expected, female statuettes are not all alike: they differ according to time and place of provenance. Nevertheless, the basic features remain the same. Female statuettes of the later, Neolithic, epoch were similarly executed in accordance with a rigid schema. Of course, this is to say little or nothing about the quality of individual works. Their quality, however, cannot be judged by modern artistic standards. Rather, we can only ask to what extent "the artist"—the maker—did justice to his theme, given the conditions under which he worked and the nature of the medium. What we may find fascinating in the formal aspects of the work was often the result of chance or accident. There is no sound basis for making an artistic comparison between the *Dame de Sireuil* and the *Venus of Willendorf,* because both are primarily objects of worship, not works of art. Artistic evaluation of such objects is necessarily ex post facto, which immediately renders any such judgment baseless. In the *Dame de Sireuil,* the convexity of the abdomen, in counterpoise to the disproportionately exaggerated buttocks, and the over-all boldness of the modeling might seem to express a conscious stylistic principle. But this is merely an illusion.

La Dame de Sireuil, statuette with head and arms missing, traces of the hair discernible on the shoulder. Translucent calcite, height $3^5/_8''$. From Sireuil (Dordogne), France. Musée des Antiquités Nationales, Saint-Germain-en-Laye

Venus of Willendorf. Limestone statuette with traces of red coloring, height 4³/₈″. From Willendorf, Wachau, Lower Austria. Naturhistorisches Museum, Vienna

Similarly, the torso may strike us as elegant, notwithstanding the cursory treatment of the legs, and may evoke latter-day modes of artistic representation. We may also be enchanted by the translucency of the stone employed. (In fact, it was probably chosen because, among other things, it is fairly easy to work.) Yet, when all this has been said, the maker's primary aim in giving the statuette such appeal as he did was to arouse realistic associations through uninhibited exaggeration of natural forms. In this respect, he achieved a little differently just what the maker of the Willendorf *Venus* achieved. Repeatedly, this and other such works have been regarded as portraitlike representations of Paleolithic women, at least of a Paleolithic "type" supposed actually to have existed. The error here is to confuse artistic with anatomical realism, when the whole point of these works was suggestion through exaggeration. Even though, in the Willendorf statuette, the kneecaps are indicated, the arms and legs and featureless face are still only secondary features. The actual visual concept is put across by the ornamental treatment of the hair, the exaggeratedly heavy breasts, and the distended belly. It is but a short step from a naturalism like this, which barely remains within the limits of the believable, to a schematization in which the female sexual characteristics completely dominate the picture, rendering superfluous any attempt at further detail (cf. page 26).

Another major motif in Paleolithic art was the representation of animals. Just like the earliest representations of people, they were not portrayed in a spirit of decoration, but to serve a specific purpose. When men depend on hunting for their livelihood, their attitude toward animals is necessarily governed by a multitude of hard and fast rules. The great number of hunting scenes in Paleolithic art cannot be accounted for by purposes of magic alone. Moreover, actual scenes of men hunting are relatively rare, and those we do have were never intended to record the particular exploits of particular hunters.

It is, however, conceivable that, even at this early date, they may have some mythological meaning: a ritual re-enactment of the first hunt, perhaps, or the exploit of some legendary ancestor. Furthermore, the primitive hunter did not look upon the animals he hunted solely as game, but as beings in possession of mysterious powers and protected by supernatural forces. This is why he did not kill without first making some sort of offering to those powers, or at least without taking measures to turn aside their wrath. For instance, he attempted to propitiate them by sacrificing a mammoth or a bear from time to time. In this way, he hoped to attain a degree of security in a world he imagined inhabited by spirits.

The finest small sculptures come from southwestern Europe, which also produced the magnificent cave paintings of animals (cf. pages 42–47). Especially noteworthy are the tools and utensils with figural decoration. Not only do they stand out among the mass of everyday objects of use, but they give us a glimpse into the Paleolithic mentality. This is particularly true of the "pierced staffs," the exact function of which is still uncertain. Mostly made of reindeer horn, they have a round hole at one end and are often provided with a hook at the other. Similar "hooks" or corresponding hollows are often found on spear throwers, which were held parallel to the spear in such a way that the tip of the shaft rested on the hook or in the hollow. The spear thrower itself was grasped by the end with the hole in it, and served as a lever to give additional speed to the spear as it is thrown. Weapons of this type were in use throughout the Early Paleolithic, but it was not until the Magdalenian period that the pierced staffs acquired their magnificent figural form. Most often they are too short and too fragile to have served for practical everyday purposes. Although they are indisputably derived from weaponry, their actual function can be inferred from certain peculiarities. For one thing, they often seem to have been deliberately (rather than accidentally) broken, as though they embodied some dangerous, or perhaps expendable, image. Moreover, the figures carved on them seem in every case to refer to specific animal species. Whether the boring of the hole had some special significance—a "magic circle," for instance— remains an open question, but all the evidence seems to indicate that the pierced staffs had some nonutilitarian function. They may have had some protective magic for the hunter, or perhaps served as insurance that the animal species would go on multiplying even though individual members of it were hunted down and killed. If so, the animal image would express a wish, a prayer; would reflect "a consummation devoutly to be wish'd." In this sense, the French term by which the pierced staffs are often designated, *bâtons de commandement,* would not be altogether inappropriate, although what it primarily evokes is the tribal chieftain's symbol of authority. Of course, at that early date, the functions of chief and witch doctor may very well have been embodied in the same individual. Be that as it may, the carved animals may also have had the function of totemic emblems, may have expressed the hunter's sense of kinship with a particular species of animal. This would account for the frequency with which the same motifs occur at a single site—the numerous bird figures at Le Mas d'Azil, for instance.

Pierced staff with carved heath cock (reconstruction). Reindeer antler, length of bird 2³/₄″. From Le Mas d'Azil (Ariège), France. Musée des Antiquités Nationales, Saint-Germain-en-Laye

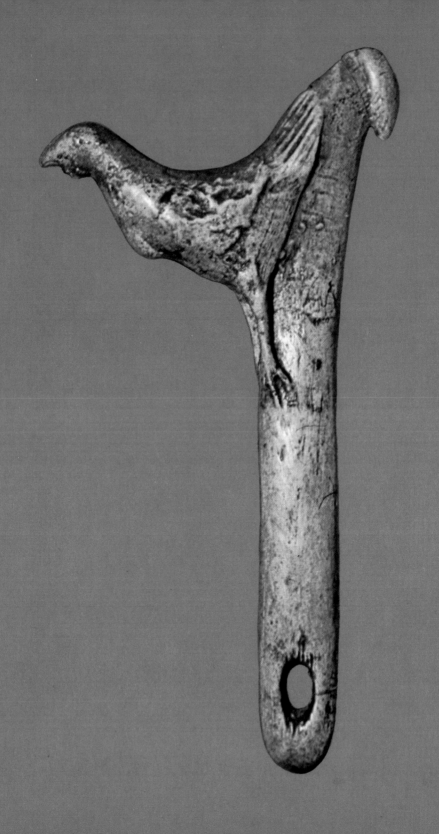

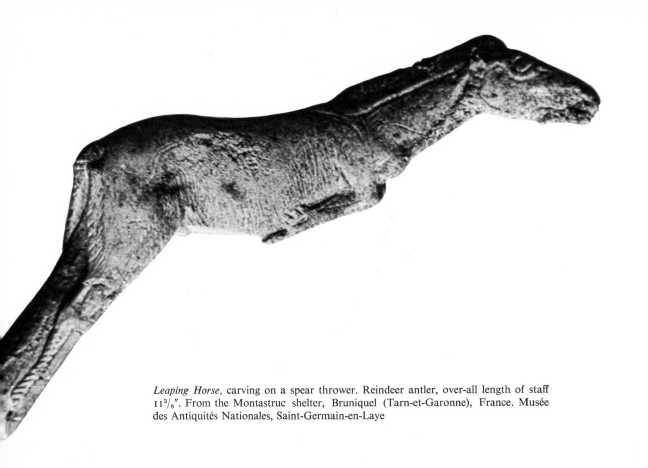

Leaping Horse, carving on a spear thrower. Reindeer antler, over-all length of staff 11³/₈″. From the Montastruc shelter, Bruniquel (Tarn-et-Garonne), France. Musée des Antiquités Nationales, Saint-Germain-en-Laye

Wild horses are frequently represented in Paleolithic small sculpture, drawing, and painting. The horse was highly esteemed as the hunter's quarry. Later, in the Neolithic period, when it was domesticated and bred as cattle are bred today, for meat, it almost entirely ceased to be represented until well into the Metal Age. It does not reappear in art until the equestrian society of Hallstatt times. By then, man's view of the world had completely changed, and he had learned to draw conceptually (cf. page 123) or was beginning to schematize (cf. page 116) and stylize (cf. pages 114, 143) under the influence of the more advanced Mediterranean civilizations. Paleolithic representations of horses are symbolic in the sense that they stand for the entire species or a particular herd, and were made in the service of magic or religion. At the same time, they are perfectly naturalistic, to a degree never achieved again in European Prehistoric art. The little ivory horse from Les Espélugues (facing page) is one of the very finest pieces to have come down to us. It looks as though it has just pulled up and is sniffing danger. The rendering of head and neck suggests careful planning and gives the impression of gracefulness achieved quite independently of the limitations of the material. The impression is deceptive, however, for Paleolithic carvers knew how to turn flaws and awkwardness in the material to their advantage. They could adapt a given motif so skillfully to the shape of their material that, in the end, a form in fact imposed on them by the material looks as though it has been deliberately planned. Here, the horse's intensely stretched-out neck was dictated by the shape of the ivory, in other words, by artistic economy. An even better example of how necessity can be turned into a virtue is the *Leaping Horse* from Montastruc (facing page). Here, the horse is carved on a spear thrower made of a reindeer antler, which hardly gave the sculptor much freedom. The hindquarters merge into the staff with the slightest bend possible, while the forelegs are tucked closely up against the animal's belly. Head and neck are stretched in the same plane as the body. Necessarily, this conveys the sense of free movement. However, the expressiveness is derived solely from the sculptor's skillful exploitation of the material's limitations. Many Paleolithic works, including paintings on irregular rock walls, exhibit the same adaptability. At the same time, of course, the sure eye and hand of the hunter, who must observe sharply and make up his mind quickly, must also have been an important factor.

Wild Horse. Ivory, length c. 3″. From Les Espélugues, Lourdes (Hautes-Pyrénées), France. Musée des Antiquités Nationales, Saint-Germain-en-Laye

Wild Horse. Engraving on the frontal bone of a horse's skull, length c. 8″. From the cave of La Mairie, Teyjat (Dordogne), France. Saint-Périer Collection, Morigny

The engraving from Teyjat also illustrates how a naturalistic representation can be adapted to almost any material. This picture of a horse was engraved with a flint blade on the frontal bone of a horse's skull. This double reference to the horse is surely not without meaning. What we have here is definitely more than a mere sketch; in fact, a number of other bone fragments and stone implements, some of them with traces of red coloring, have been found at the same site. Though no masterpiece, the drawing is skillfully placed between the eye cavities, so as to make use of the largest possible surface. Another kind of artistic economy can be observed in the small horse's head from Isturitz (facing page). Here, the ears are not fully executed, appear pasted onto the skull, and are set too low. Because the artist worked the stone with stone implements, he therefore had to try to keep the figure within the block form and to rely on low relief for the rendering of all details. Animal bones are, of course, easier to work with.

24

No wonder, then, that many animal heads are executed in the silhouette technique, particularly horses carved from bone fragments. The lines and hatchings over the muzzle of the horse from Arudy (right) do not represent any sort of harness but are a schematic treatment of the muscles and tendons that set off the different parts. Such animal heads are usually pierced, thus identifying them as pendants. They were probably worn as amulets.

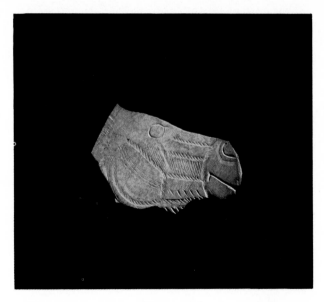

Head of a Horse. Reindeer antler, length $1^3/_4''$. From the Espalungue cave, Arudy (Basses-Pyrénées), France. Musée des Antiquités Nationales, Saint-Germain-en-Laye

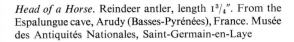

Head of a Horse. Limestone, height $3^1/_8''$. From Isturitz (Basses-Pyrénées), France. Saint-Périer Collection, Morigny

25

Female Idols (highly stylized). Ivory, height $3^{1}/_{4}''$ and $3^{3}/_{8}''$. From Dolní Věstonice, Mikulov, Moravia, Czechoslovakia. Moravian Museum, Brno

Head of an Ibex. Relief carving on a bone staff, length 10⅝". From Le Mas d'Azil (Ariège), France. Musée des Antiquités Nationales, Saint-Germain-en-Laye

Head of an Ibex. Engraving on a bone staff, length 5⅛". From Isturitz (Basses-Pyrénées), France. Saint-Périer Collection, Morigny

One of the most frequently represented animals in Paleolithic art is the ibex. On one hooked staff from Le Mas d'Azil, it is in such low relief as to be recognizable only thanks to the more deeply carved horns. Such extreme respect for the object's shape and function is frequently met with and surely marks the terminal stage of a stylistic evolution which, over and over again, leads from realism to schematization, from the mirror image of reality to the symbolic sign. Engravings continue to be naturalistic where there is enough room for them. The ibex on the rounded staff from Isturitz, however, has to share the limited space with a strip of zigzag decoration. Just what is represented at the bottom of our second example is not quite clear—perhaps they are human legs painted or tattooed, or wound about with thongs. Of course, here we can give only a few examples of the trend away from naturalism to schematization, nor are our examples in proper chronological order. Moreover, the human figure seems to have begun to be schematized quite early. From the period preceding the Magdalenian, we find female figures reduced to a single sexual characteristic, as in the staff-shaped female figures from Dolní Věstonice (facing page). The development from realistic representation to a sign, and from that to purely symbolic forms, probably reflects some profound change in Paleolithic conceptions of the world.

Detail of a club with engraving of a stylized human figure. Deer antler, over-all length of the club c. 17″. From a bog at Jordløse, Zealand, Denmark. Nationalmuseet, Copenhagen

In some instances, the difference between the naturalism of a hunting mentality and later modes of drawing is also geographically determined. In the engraving from Le Mas d'Azil (facing page), the human figure still appears in an entirely realistic setting. Although the face is not executed in detail, the figure cannot be mistaken for anything but a human being, for it walks erect and carries a stick over one shoulder. All we can make out of the rest of this fragment is a single paw of a bear. So far as comparison with the lifeless schematic figure from Jordløse (left) goes, it makes no difference whether the engraving represents a fight between man and bear, the carrying home of game, or some ritual celebration. No matter what, we are sure that the action represented really took place, whereas the Jordløse figure stands stiff and uninvolved between geometric shapes and ornamentation. The latter work does not reflect some independent evolution of Paleolithic-Mesolithic stylistic forms in Scandinavia, but a general trend toward schematization. As it goes on, regional features develop, such as we find in late cave paintings in northeastern Spain (page 49). When, toward the close of the Paleolithic period (the seventh and sixth millenniums B.C.), the ice drew back farther and farther north, the arctic fauna migrated northward and was followed by the reindeer hunters whose existence depended on the great herds of wild animals. In this way, the southern traditions of drawing reached northern Europe, where they apparently continued to evolve into the schematized rock drawings of the Neolithic period (cf. pages 56, 57). The comparative isolation of the northern hunting grounds one from another inevitably gave rise to regional peculiarities: for instance, the use of heavy dotted lines and the practice of outlining the human figures with a double line. Also, the signs and ornamental devices take on forms of their own, but the row of lozenges seen here at the left of the human figure (in this photograph only half is visible, giving the impression of a chevron stripe) belongs to the common European stock of patterns.

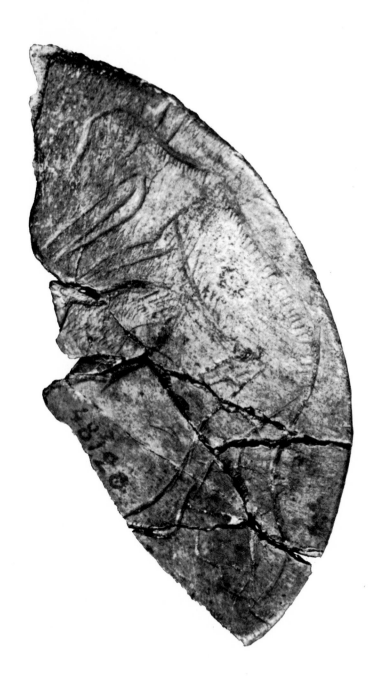

Man and Bear. Engraved bone fragment, height c. 3″. From Le Mas d'Azil (Ariège), France. Musée des Antiquités Nationales, Saint-Germain-en-Laye

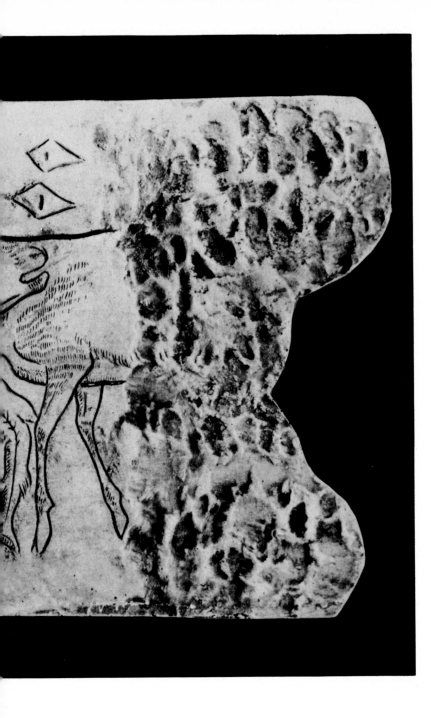

Group scenes are, for the most part, confined to herds of animals in movement. The background they move against is rarely indicated, or at best suggested, as in the swimming deer at Lascaux (page 45). Perspective rendering was, of course, not yet possible. Instead, a combination of the direct visual image and empirical impressions expresses the inner meaning. On the engraved staff from Lortet, the fish and the deer seem arbitrarily juxtaposed; however, it was probably the artist's intention to show that the deer are crossing a stream, using fish to suggest the latter. Not that an actual stream is portrayed, but to hunters and fishermen, fish are inevitably associated with running water. The two geometric signs (over the animal at the right) may refer to a particular place, even to a particular event, though it is impossible to decipher them.

Stags (or *Reindeer*) *Crossing a Stream with Fish,* impression rolled from an engraved staff. Reindeer antler, length $9^3/_4''$. From Lortet (Hautes-Pyrénées), France. Musée des Antiquités Nationales, Saint-Germain-en-Laye

Mammoth, with additional exploratory lines. Ivory, length 3³/₄″. From the Obere Klausen-höhle, Neuessing, Kelheim, Bavaria, Germany. Prähistorische Staatssammlung, Munich

Mammoth, carving from the end of a pierced staff. Reindeer antler, length c. 5″. From ▶ the Montastruc shelter, Bruniquel (Tarn-et-Garonne), France. British Museum, London

Independently of its magical functions, Paleolithic art depicts the fauna that actually existed in the period, though not all species known to have existed are portrayed. Not surprisingly, the animals that were especially important to human life were given preference. Big game was most frequently depicted, beginning with the mammoth, the largest of the Ice Age hunter's prey. Its appearance is naturally bound to the cold phases of the last glacial epoch. By the time cave painting was at its peak, the mammoth was no longer represented. The ivory plaque from Neuessing (facing page) displays a number of drawings superposed on one another, but the central motif is unmistakable. The largest of all animals is outlined with a few strokes, and the movement of the legs is clearly indicated. The shagginess of the creature's hair is shown on belly and head. The upper edge of the fragment provides the outline of the animal's back and the top of its head, as in the carved-silhouette technique.

The man who carved the mammoth on the pierced staff from Montastruc was even more limited by the shape of his material. Although he skillfully combined tusks and trunk, so that it looks as though the animal's head is raised in anger, so little room was left for the legs that he could only render them close together.

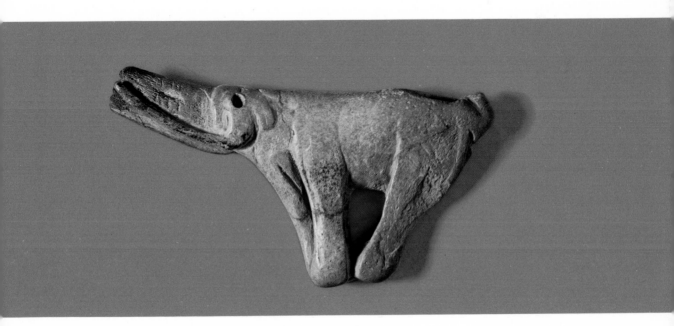

Bison. Reindeer antler, length 4″. From La Madeleine, Tursac (Dordogne), France. Musée des Antiquités Nationales, Saint-Germain-en-Laye

Bisons were frequently represented. In the low relief from La Madeleine (above), a single bison is forcefully portrayed, although it is not correctly proportioned. The powerful neck and hindquarters endow the animal with a certain massiveness, as does the way the head is turned back against the body. The horns could not be made to stand out from the flat surface, but the artist managed to incorporate them in the relief, although in false perspective.

Reindeer and other kinds of deer must have been especially abundant, for representations of these animals are numerous. Moreover, antlers provided the material from which many implements were fashioned. Engravings of such animals include some vivid naturalistic portrayals in no way inferior to the cave paintings. In the example shown at the foot of the facing page, the fluid movement of the two reindeer is rendered with the aid of the irregularities of the horn on which they were carved. Just because the animals are shown one behind the other we should not presume any ornamental intention; rather, what we have here is a vivid miniature based on real-life models.

34

Galloping Stag. Engraved stone plaque, width 4³/₄″. From the shelter of La Garenne, Saint-Marcel (Indre), France. Musée des Antiquités Nationales, Saint-Germain-en-Laye

Two Reindeer, in apparently ornamental arrangement. Reindeer antler, length 8⁵/₈″. From the Montastruc shelter, Bruniquel (Tarn-et-Garonne), France. British Museum, London

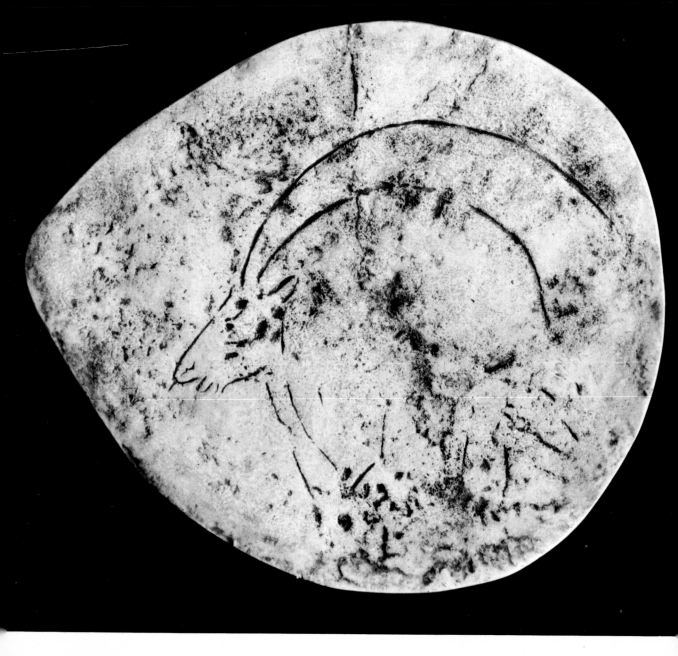

Ibex, with exaggeratedly long horns. Engraved stone plaque. Fragment of the figural decoration in the cave of La Mouthe, Les Eyzies-de-Tayac (Dordogne), France. Musée des Antiquités Nationales, Saint-Germain-en-Laye

Fighting Ibexes. Low relief on one of the decorated stones that stood in a semicircle around what was probably some kind of ▶ sanctuary, width 43¹/₄". From the shelter of Le Roc de Sers (Charente), France. Musée des Antiquités Nationales, Saint-Germain-en-Laye

From the entrance to the cave of La Mouthe a corridor extends for over two hundred yards, the walls and ceiling of which are covered with figural engravings. From among these comes the head of an ibex (facing page), which attracts attention by the elegant stylization of the horns. The head itself, complete with beard, is drawn in so few lines as to look like a delicate but exact pen drawing. The engravings show that this portion of the cave was set apart as a place of worship or assembly. Such a place was also set apart in the shelter of Le Roc de Sers, where several stone blocks decorated with low reliefs formed a semicircle; originally, they probably stood on a base at the back of the rock shelter. They had already been damaged when discovered, and the decorated sides lay face down. Some lay on the slope in front of the rock overhang. It would appear that this had been an old place of worship, destroyed at some later period which regarded such images as the work of the devil. The figures include six pregnant horses, bisons, and several ibexes. One slab shows a little man with a stick over his shoulder pursued by a musk ox. The most vivid scene is that of two ibexes locking horns. Needless to say, this is not a matter of mere decoration, but of representation undoubtedly related to the purposes served by the cave.

The first regularly shaped figure to have been discovered seems to have been the circle. Red-colored dots and circles appear on cave walls in many localities. They vary considerably in size and are often combined with other signs. What they signified, alone or in combination, has mostly remained a mystery. That the rows of dots in the cave known as the Obere Klausenhöhle must have stood for something can be inferred from the way they are arranged. That they are colored also suggests that they had some important significance: the use of red chalk or ocher long played a great part in magic and worship. There are traces of red chalk on many female statuettes, and ocher was used in connection with human burials and animal sacrifices, either deep in the caves or at the cave entrances. The mere fact that ocher is a coloring matter widely and readily available in nature does not suffice to account for its use in Prehistoric art. Clearly, a color symbolism—not unconcerned with psychological effects—developed at an early period. In any case, the color red seems from the outset to have been associated with birth, fertility, and burial rites, in keeping with a conception of life according to which birth and death are the two poles of existence and are, therefore, essentially one and the same.

Plaquette with painted red-ocher motif. Limestone, length 5³/₄″. From the Obere Klausenhöhle, Neuessing, Kelheim, Bavaria, Germany. Prähistorische Staatssammlung, Munich

Pebbles with painted geometric designs in red ocher. From Le Mas d'Azil (Ariège), France. Musée des Antiquités Nationales, Saint-Germain-en-Laye

The geometric drawings in red ocher on pebbles dating from the close of the Paleolithic period have sometimes been thought to represent a pictographic script comparable to Egyptian hieroglyphics. The comparison is surely farfetched in any literal sense, yet we can observe how the naturalistic drawings of the early hunters gradually become more schematic as we approach the Mesolithic period, particularly in southwestern Europe. In southern Spain, for example, red paintings on rock gradually froze into rigidly conventional images, into almost geometrical figures of man and animal. The earlier pictures derived from direct visual impressions gave way to more abstract representations which, in the terminal phase of this development, look like symbolic signs. The extremely simple designs on the pebbles from Le Mas d'Azil, however, go even a step further, and for this reason are virtually undecipherable.

It is hard to decide whether the Late Paleolithic incised geometric patterns on bone and ivory pendants are pure ornament, schematized figural drawings, or identification marks. The fact that they are regularly repeated suggests ornamentation; the fact that they appear in different arrangements might indicate some hidden meaning. Their possible intention remains extremely uncertain, however, for technical variations occur, and to what extent something like aesthetic standards were involved remains an open question. The patterns are not related to the shape of the objects on which they are drawn or incised, although they are naturally limited by the available surface. The same motifs could have been planned and executed on any material of any size or shape. The evidence seems to show that a playful element first made its appearance in art with these geometric incisions. The fact that the same patterns recur would not be incompatible with this hypothesis, so long as their combinations are constantly varied (cf. page 28).

Pendant with incised geometric decoration. Ivory, length 3⁷/₈″. From Předmostí, Přerov, Moravia, Czechoslovakia. Moravian Museum, Brno

Pendants with incised geometric decoration. Bone, length c. 4¹/₂″. From Marsoulas (Haute-Garonne), France. Musée des Antiquités Nationales, Saint-Germain-en-Laye

The Lascaux cave, discovered in 1940 by two local boys, contains important paintings executed in glowing colors. The natural background is almost white, so that the paintings stand out in vigorous reds, yellows, browns, and blacks (see also pages 44–46). Just inside the entrance, the Rotunda is a vaulted hall some thirty yards long by ten wide. It is also known as the "Hall of Bulls," after the monumental paintings of these animals on its walls. The largest of them is almost eighteen feet long. These figures partly cover older drawings of red-colored bovines, which apparently date from the same time as the small stags (also red) between the two large bulls. Their hoofs and horns are shown in false perspective, twisted around into the plane of the body—a characteristic of the so-called Aurignacian and Perigordian styles. The most recent of the figures are the horses in dark reddish-brown and black, which partly cover the black bulls. The strange creature at the extreme left, the so-called unicorn, comes closest to resembling a bovine or a rhinoceros, but the small head with the straight horns suggests a mythical beast. It might also represent men in animal disguise, either hunting or performing hunting magic.

Paintings on the left wall of the Rotunda in the cave at Lascaux, Montignac (Dordogne), France

◀ Paintings in the Axial Gallery of the cave at Lascaux

Paintings in the Passageway and Nave at Lascaux

The lateral galleries known as the Passageway and the Nave lead off from the right side of the Rotunda to a slightly higher part of the cave, where engravings predominate. Of the paintings, the most important is a frieze of five stags about sixteen feet across. Their necks and heads strain upward as though the animals were swimming. The placing of the work—over a recess in the wall that provides a natural "frame" at the bottom —shows skill and forethought. Here, the artist is unmistakably reproducing something that he has actually seen—the picture is genuinely "intuitive."

◀ The Axial Gallery is twenty yards long and leads down from the back of the Rotunda deep into the side of the hill. Here, paintings of bovines alternate with paintings of horses. On the facing page, a large bull is shown running above a frieze of black horses toward a branched sign. It is painted in black over older red figures. The shaggy ponies seem to be pregnant.

Paintings on the ceiling of the Axial Gallery at Lascaux. A quadrangular sign, several variations of which occur in this cave, appears between the three cows and the horses

Horses and bulls are the main motifs on the ceiling of the long Axial Gallery at Lascaux. Between the two groups, a quadrangular, gridlike sign appears, which may represent a hunter's trap. As is customary in this early painting, the horns are drawn in false perspective.

The no less famous cave of Altamira contains masterpieces of a later stage in the development of Franco-Cantabrian painting. This cave cuts through solid limestone to a distance of three hundred yards. Paintings

Standing Bison (detail). Over-all length c. 6′. On the Painted Ceiling at Altamira, Santillana, Santander, Spain ▶

and engravings appear rather haphazardly on the walls. The most magnificent of these paintings, however, are to be seen on the so-called Painted Ceiling some thirty yards from the entrance. Only bisons are represented here. The figures vary in length between about fifty-five and seventy inches, and some of the outlines are incised as well as painted. To endow the pictures with a maximum of realism, the natural irregularities of the surface are often incorporated into the painting to bring out one or another feature of the animal bodies. The pigments used are charcoal (for black) and red, yellow, and brown ocher. Remnants of chalk have been discovered among the archaeological finds on the cave floor.

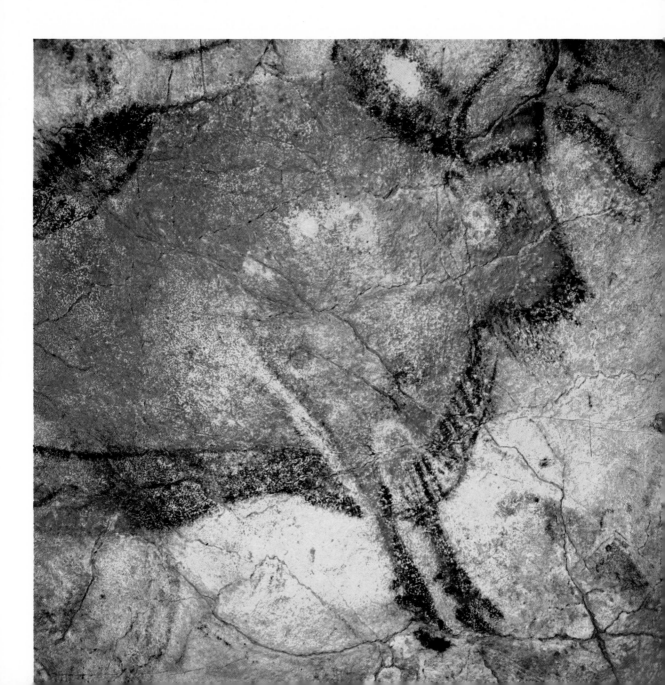

On the walls of the Gargas cave are over one hundred and fifty so-called negative imprints of hands surrounded by red or black pigment. In other caves, "positive" imprints are found, usually of the right hand: at Gargas they are mostly of the left. The pigment around them was blown over the hands, either by mouth or with the help of some hollow tube. This is clear from the fine-grained quality of the color. Occasionally, one or more finger joints are missing. This is generally ascribed to voluntary mutilation such as primitive peoples have been known to practice for a variety of reasons. Accordingly, the imprints are interpreted as a kind of personal mark, perhaps as a binding promise given either to supernatural powers or to the tribe as a whole.

Negative imprints of hands surrounded by red and black pigment.
In the cave of Gargas, Aventignan (Hautes-Pyrénées), France

Running Archer (the head and another drawing underneath this one have faded in the course of time). Distance between the feet 15³/₄″. Painting in the cave of the Val del Charco del Agua Amarga, near Alcañiz, Teruel, Spain

Recently, however, the "mutilated" fingers have been interpreted as hunting signals, as representing gestures exchanged between hunters in order not to disturb their quarry by speaking. However that may be, the peculiar imprints are obviously expressive of a more complicated mode of thinking than is elsewhere disclosed in pictorial representations of this period. How the one kind of expression developed out of the other is well illustrated in the rock paintings found in the Spanish Levant. They are postglacial and date from the Mesolithic period. Like earlier rock drawings, they are basically naturalistic, but exhibit a strong tendency toward stylization. The archer in the Agua Amarga cave, shown running in pursuit of his quarry, is a figural drawing reduced to the simplest lines. The realistic image of an earlier time, based on straightforward observation of the familiar world, has here been converted by conscious reflection into a picture of a general idea, the purpose of which is to represent an event by the simplest possible means. At least in so far as pictorial representation is concerned, such conscious abstraction indicates that man has taken a step forward toward asserting his freedom from that very nature whose outer manifestations had held him captive for so long.

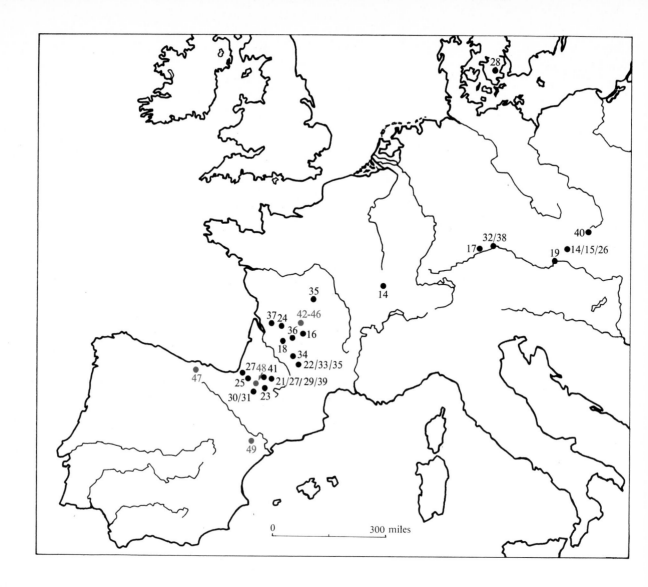

Paleolithic and Mesolithic sites

Red: cave paintings.

This map does not reflect the actual distribution of Paleolithic and Mesolithic peoples, the sites indicated being only those relevant to the illustrations in this book. Since the most numerous and best-preserved Paleolithic remains are to be found in natural caves, the emphasis falls on the areas where these are found. It is, however, true that finds from the Pyrenees and the Dordogne represent a real focal point of Paleolithic art, favored by the southern climate, despite the limited number of actual sites so far discovered.

50

Chronological chart of the Paleolithic and Mesolithic periods

The numbers refer to pages. Where the dating is uncertain, a question mark has been added to the page reference. The red shading provides an approximate idea of the duration of the industry to which the finds listed belong.

This highly simplified schema covers only the last millenniums of the fourth glacial period, which began about 120,000 years before Christ. Scientific methods supply the basis for the dating, but many details are still debated. No attempt has been made to standardize the terminology. The names of the different groups derive from French archaeological sites at which typical ensembles of artifacts were discovered. Such names, therefore, do not designate particular periods, but specific forms of stone and bone implements. The relative chronology of the various industries in contiguous cultural strata can sometimes be quite accurately established, but generally disturbances of one kind or another have altered the original picture. The wide diffusion of many groups provides other problems, making it difficult to determine whether they succeeded one another or coexisted. Some were undoubtedly coexistent, and the East Gravettian industry in particular seems to have extended over a long period. Thus, the assigning of exact dates is beset with difficulties. It is agreed that the transition from the Paleolithic to the Mesolithic took place between 10,000 and 6000 B.C.—but precisely when varies from place to place. In Scandinavia, living conditions did not become tolerable until the icecap had retreated. Here, dwelling sites in open country provide names for the various groups.

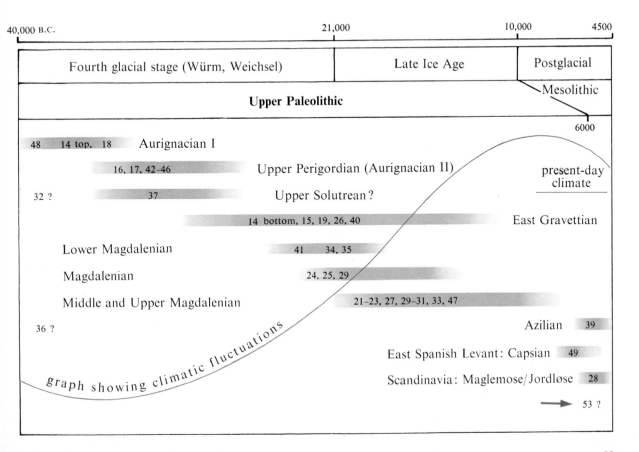

Club in the shape of an elk's head. Stone, length 8¼". From Alunda, Uppland, Sweden. Statens Historiska Museum, Stockholm

THE NEOLITHIC PERIOD

The various regions of Europe attained the Neolithic stage of civilization at very different times. What has been called the "cultural fault" running from the southeast to the west and north of Europe, resulted in a temporal lag which was also reflected in the arts and crafts. The technological and economic achievements of the Neolithic age in Europe were all based upon borrowings from the ancient civilizations of the eastern Mediterranean. The most important of these achievements were methods of constructing dwellings, animal husbandry, cultivation, the making of pottery utensils, and new ways of working stone. These cultural advances did not always reach a given region simultaneously. Some were brought by new settlers, others came about through contacts between hitherto separate groups. In this connection, the Danube served as a particularly important early link between the Mediterranean world and Central Europe. A later route of cultural dissemination lay along the Mediterranean coastline westward to the Iberian Peninsula, and from there northward along the Atlantic to western France, to the British Isles, and—eventually, during the Bronze Age—as far as Scandinavia, a border area from which the ice receded comparatively late. Mesolithic and even Paleolithic ways of life lasted much longer in the North than elsewhere. How such profound differences in levels of cultural development can coexist in a single region is even today illustrated by the Lapps in the far Scandinavian North. Although they have long since learned how to control a given animal species, rather than to hunt it down indiscriminately, they are, nevertheless, still just as dependent upon the reindeer as were the hunters of Paleolithic times to whom it never occurred to keep herds and who probably would not have been capable of doing so in any case.

The introduction of agriculture and animal husbandry was inevitably reflected in the appearance of new motifs in art. However, in the Scandinavian peninsula and in neighboring Karelia, representations of wild animals occur in numbers only conceivable as the products of a society still at the hunting and food-gathering stage (cf. page 56). Among the choicer examples of small carvings are stone clubs that have been given the shape of an elk's head; these probably served both as weapons and as insignia of rank. Carved out of slate or some other stone and then polished, they compare not unfavorably with both naturalistic and stylized Paleolithic works of western Europe, though they certainly date from a much later period. The little amber horse from Woldenberg (page 55) also seems to continue the tradition of Paleolithic realism. However, the impulse to ornamentation is more marked here, though only in the form of rows of dots. Articulation of the surface by repetition of the same or similar signs and patterns is even more clearly discernible in an amber pendant in the shape of an elk's head (below, bottom right). Here, the ornamentation has no functional relation to the object on which it appears; its purpose is merely to embellish the surface. Since amber is a translucent substance, this also involves effects of light and shadow.

Amber carvings from Denmark. Top left: *Bear;* length c. 2³/₄″; from Resen, Zealand. Bottom right: pendant in the shape of an elk's head; length c. 2¹/₂″; from Egemarke, Zealand. Top right and bottom left: ornamented pendants. Nationalmuseet, Copenhagen

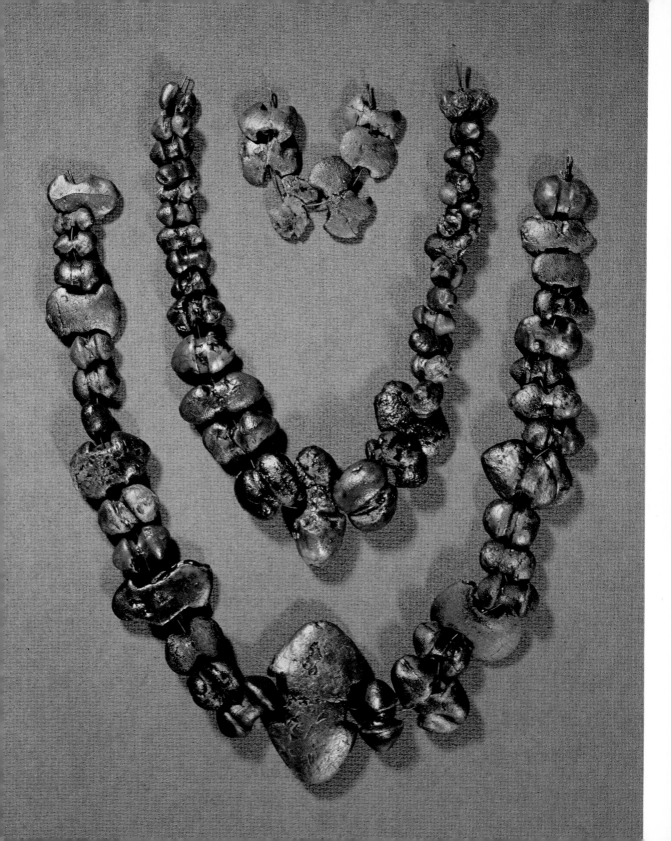

◀ Necklaces with beads shaped like clubs and double axes. Amber, length of the axheads $^7/_8$–$2^3/_8$″. From a megalithic barrow at Graese, Zealand, Denmark. Nationalmuseet, Copenhagen

Horse. Amber, length $4^3/_4$″. From Woldenberg, Friedeberg, Brandenburg, Germany. Museum für Vor- und Frühgeschichte, Berlin

At all periods of Prehistory, articles of personal adornment, including amulets, were made out of amber. Deposits on the southern shores of the Baltic Sea were being drawn upon during the Neolithic age; but trade in amber should not be overestimated, for similar deposits were also being exploited in southern and eastern Europe. Amber was frequently used for amulets and other objects of adornment supposed to possess magical powers: apparently, special virtues were ascribed to this rare and beautiful substance. The beads shaped like clubs and double axes in the necklaces from Denmark (facing page) have a symbolic significance which was obviously enhanced when they were made of amber.

Rock drawings (the schematized figures of humans, bears, and elks have been filled in with chalk). Now situated c. 60′ above sea level, due to the rising of the coast during the postglacial period. Skavberg, on the Tromsø Sound, southwest of Tromsø, Norway

Rock drawings are found in varying density from the west coast of Norway into northwestern Russia. Treated in various styles, the motifs reflect the life of Neolithic fishermen and hunters (cf. page 52). Most of the outlines were pecked out, some were ground in, a few were painted. The drawing goes to the point of extreme schematization. Subjects treated are primarily the larger game animals such as reindeer and bears, but fish and seals are also included. Occasional human figures are characterized as hunters by their bows and spears. Most of the sites where such drawings occur lie on fjords, on the banks of rivers, along the shores of lakes, or near waterfalls and rapids. These are places where animals still come today for water and good fishing spots are to be found.

Detail of the illustration above. Height of the figures 27⁵/₈″ and 25¹/₄″ ▶

The Early Neolithic clay female statuettes found in the Danube Valley obviously represent the same type of figure as the Paleolithic statuettes. In form, they derive from preclassical Mediterranean works. Like the numerous marble figurines that have been found in the Cyclades, they are highly stylized; though small, the breasts are clearly emphasized, hips and thighs exaggeratedly so. The markedly tapering legs of the originals are often reduced to thick stumps. Similarly, the characteristic Mediterranean arm gesture has degenerated into a simple lateral position. Just as with the Paleolithic figures, the face (with few exceptions) is only roughly indicated. There can be no doubt that these statuettes represent a mother-goddess, such as was known in lands bordering the Mediterranean by many names and in many forms. Over one hundred such figurines have been found in the village of Střelice alone, some of them broken into small pieces. Like painted Moravian pottery, they hark back, stylistically, to southeastern originals (cf. page 64). Not all the statuettes, however, seem to be

local reproductions. The limestone cult figure from Asia Minor discovered in southern Germany (page 62) suggests that imports from the eastern Mediterranean occasionally reached Central Europe.

Female Idols. Clay, height 8⅝″ and 8¼″. From Střelice, Znojmo, Moravia, Czechoslovakia. Moravian Museum, Brno

Female Idol. Clay, height 6″. From Střelice, Znojmo, Moravia, Czechoslovakia. Moravian Museum, Brno

Neck of a jar with representation of a human face. Clay, diameter at top 5^1/$_2$″. From Stuttgart-Bad Cannstatt, Germany. Württembergisches Landesmuseum, Stuttgart

Pottery opened up new opportunities for figural representation. It is probably no accident that human figures appear from the outset in drawings and reliefs; though highly schematized, such figures are not just there as decoration. Occasionally their features seem quite expressive, but this could not have been intended and is merely the result of the maker's lack of skill. The face on the neck of a jar from Stuttgart-Bad Cannstatt (above) seems to be smiling. However, this impression is produced simply by a deep line that runs beneath the nose and below the very unartistic round hollows which indicate the eyes. Similarly, the figure in relief on the clay kettle from Gneiding (facing page) was certainly not intended to look like a demon, as it might seem to us. Here, the expressiveness is due to clumsy handling of the material: it was probably by pure accident that the lump of clay first took on a human appearance.

Kettle with human figure in relief. Clay, height of kettle 9⁷/₈″, of the figure 3¹/₈″. From Gneiding, Landau an der Isar, Bavaria, Germany. Prähistorische Staatssammlung, Munich

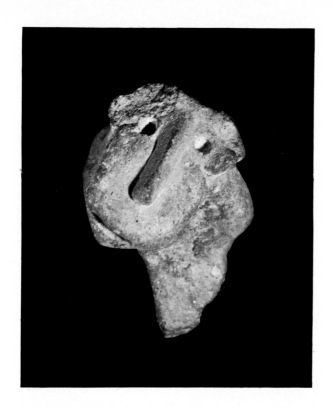

Human Head, on broken-off handle from the lid of a pot. Clay, length 2¹/₄″. From Kostelec, Prostějov, Moravia, Czechoslovakia. Museum, Olomouc

Cult figure from Asia Minor in schematized human form. Limestone, height 2⁷/₈″. From Dietenhausen, Oberlahn, Hesse, Germany. Museum, Wiesbaden
▼

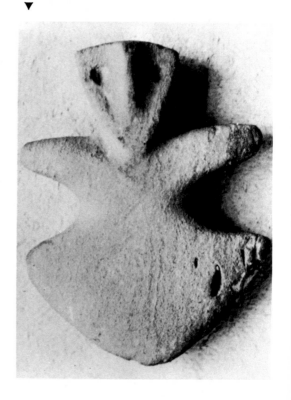

Needless to say, the figural representations of human beings do not invariably go back to eastern Mediterranean models. In many instances, neither the content nor the stylistic origin of such representations can be established. This is especially true of small sculptures, which only too often owe their shaping to chance. The aggrieved expression of the clay head from Kostelec is one such pseudo effect. There is no such thing as a Prehistoric art of portraiture; invariably, there is a schematic model which may or may not be successfully followed. All the little clay face is intended to denote is a creature of human shape, but we have no way of knowing whether, in this instance, the potter was merely clumsy or, perhaps, was copying some foreign model. The cult figure from Asia Minor found at Dietenhausen may have served as such a model. In this figure, everything is reduced to a schema which seems at once simple and ingenious. The almost triangular head is given life

62

Female Idol, in the form of a jar, with traces of white and red paint. Clay, height 16³/₄". From a mound (tell) at Vidra, Bucharest, Romania. National Museum of Antiquities, Bucharest

by indications of nose and eyes. Prehistoric art learned such masterly stylization from the Orient, except for those cases where the Nordic animal representations (cf. pages 52, 53, 55) had translated the simplified Paleolithic realism into a stylistic form. On this score, every geographical area learned its own lessons. Thus, in the northeast of the Balkan Peninsula, we find some rather homely sculptures, such as the female clay figure from Vidra. Nothing about it suggests that the site was fairly close to the more advanced Mediterranean cultures. The Balkan potter dressed up the beautiful nakedness of his prototypes with a hodgepodge of ornamental lines representing a barbaric mixture of textile patterns, personal ornaments, and perhaps also tattooing.

Painted pottery. Left: part of the neck of a pot; height 5″; from Střelice, Znojmo. Right: ladle; length 6″; from Ctidručice, Moravské Budejovice, Moravia, Czechoslovakia. Moravian Museum, Brno

Many relics of Neolithic culture cannot be adequately interpreted because they cannot be accurately dated. Consequently, we cannot be sure where they originated or, subsequently, where their influence was felt. In this connection, the products of the Middle and Lower Danube Valley are greatly overestimated. While there is no doubt that these regions repeatedly played the part of intermediary between the advanced civilizations of the eastern Mediterranean and the parts of Europe still at Prehistoric stages of development, still, neither in the Neolithic period nor in the period immediately following did they make any very important contribution of their own. By contrast, western and northern Europe reacted to Mediterranean stimuli in highly original ways, giving rise to new forms and new styles. In some cases, they resisted new ideas and new techniques. Painted pottery is a good example: it never spread north or west of southeastern Europe. Elsewhere, the ordinary incised and grooved ornamentation affirmed itself, adapted to the shape of the vessel and, at most, accentuated by inlays of white material. When we come to painted ceramics, we are confronted with an entirely new medium which is applied to the smooth surface in accordance with new stylistic laws. Whether such painting would or could have arisen without the prior existence of figurative and ornamental work on fairly large surfaces remains an open question. However, painted vessels were produced as early as Predynastic Egypt. Neolithic painted pottery reached a high point of development in the Tripolye culture of southern

Russia, probably stimulated by Near Eastern influences. The flowing volute spirals of North Romanian examples, such as those from Cucuteni, characterize a particularly flourishing period in the development of ceramic painting. On the other hand, the painted pottery of Moravia, quite apart from the problems of dating, strikes us as a stunted growth, an escape into the very simplest geometric forms.

Female Idol and painted jar. Clay. From Cucuteni-Băiceni, Jassy, Romania. National Museum of Antiquities, Bucharest

Female Idols, in schematized human form. Clay, height c. 8″, c. 5″, and c. 6³/₄″. From Bronze Age urn burials at Cîrna, Dolj, Romania. National Museum of Antiquities, Bucharest

Consistent schematization of the human figure necessarily overlaps with, or spills over into, ornamentation. This was especially true in southeastern Europe. The clay sculpture from Vadastra (facing page) looks more like a miniature votive temple than a human figure. The rings around its neck are certainly reminiscent of earlier naturalistic representations. The head is geometrically stylized, the body completely devoid of articulation. The incised ornament probably corresponds to a secret symbolism. The meanders on the chest suggest a labyrinthine maze—the labyrinth always has cosmogonic significance in myths and fairy tales, that is, refers to an idea of universal order. Stylization of this type is not purely of the artist's choice or invention. In the case of sacred objects, artists are subject to rigorous tradition and specific features are clung to for centuries, long after the original meaning has been forgotten. Thus, the peculiar posture of the Bronze Age idols from Cîrna goes back to a Neolithic tradition (cf. page 63). The same is true of their costume, as is indicated by the incised pattern. The statuettes, placed as offerings in urn burials, obviously represent either a goddess of death or a woman presiding over funerary rites. What we have here is probably a blend of barbaric and classical conceptions, as also in the clay figure from Dupljaja (page 146). This conjecture is supported by the stylized bell-shaped skirt, which goes back to Cretan-Mycenaean costumes. Its recent interpretation as a priest's robe, i.e., a man's garb, rests upon an ill-considered analogy with modern costume.

Idol, in schematized human form. Clay. From Vadastra, Romanati, Romania. National Museum of Antiquities, Bucharest

Animal-shaped jar with funnel-shaped neck. Clay, length 7⁷/₈″. From Abrahám, Slovakia. Museum, Piešťany

As might be expected, representations of domesticated animals are not lacking among the peasant cultures of the Neolithic era, though it is often hard to determine accurately from the surviving clay fragments to which species the animals belonged. A number of cow-shaped vessels appear among the earliest examples of *Bandkeramik* (pottery with curvilinear decoration); a few shapeless pots seem to represent pigs. But what animal the vessel with a funnel-shaped neck from Abrahám in Slovakia may represent is hard to decide. The conventional interpretation as a bear is based on the rather superficial assumption that the Neolithic potter was primarily concerned with anatomical accuracy. Most likely, he intended a symbolic image. Similarly, the two-headed goat from Kroměříž (facing page) can hardly be regarded as the literal imitation of a real animal. Apart from whatever special functions this animal sculpture had (which may be indicated by the hole in the back), the basic consideration here is the fact that the piece has the shape of a goat. Whether the twin heads have symbolic significance remains uncertain: since we are not dealing here with animal representation in the usual sense, it is virtually impossible to find a clue as to the artist's intention. However, for all their artistic deficiencies, animal-shaped vessels and animal sculptures cannot be classified as ordinary pottery; like vessels with human figures, they were not destined for everyday use.

68

Two-Headed Goat, with hole in the back. Clay, height 5″. From Kroměříž, Moravia, Czechoslovakia. Moravian Museum, Brno

Pierced-lug beaker and collared flask, examples of northern megalithic *Tiefstichkeramik*. From a long barrow at Drouwen, Drente, Holland. Rijksmuseum, Leiden

Funnel beaker, hanging vessel, and pierced-lug beaker. ▶ Northern megalithic *Tiefstichkeramik*. From Denmark, the hanging vessel from Høbjerg, Zealand. Nationalmuseet, Copenhagen

Classification of the numerous Neolithic tribes or peoples rests largely upon finds of pottery vessels which were placed in their graves, filled with food and drink. Because such vessels were accompanied by other articles, we can determine what sort of shapes and styles of decoration characterized a given period. All Neolithic pottery was fashioned by hand, the potter's wheel being still unknown. There are many forms and patterns, and the main types all have many local variants. For instance, the northern megalithic cultures produced funnel beakers, pierced-lug beakers, hanging vessels, and collared flasks. Danish specimens are always somewhat different from the Dutch. What both have in common with pottery from other regions is the deeply incised decoration *(Tiefstichornament)*, executed with a pointed stick and generally filled in with white pigment. Only in this way was the decoration, spread out over the dark surface of the pot, fully effective. This early decorative art was related to, and emphasized, the structure of the vessel. By contrast, in the Late Neolithic rapport patterns, the only slightly articulated surface is included in the ornament through the reserving of certain areas or the dividing of it into zones. On the rims of many bell beakers, the triangular unfilled spaces form the same pattern as the incised triangles, namely, a zigzag which looks the same whether viewed from above or below (page 73).

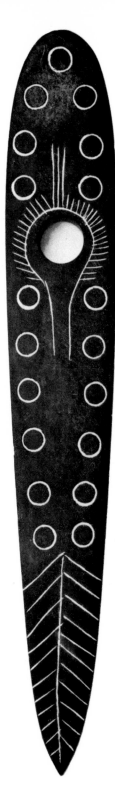

Ceremonial axes with engraved symbolic signs. Stone. From Halle-Radewell (left) and Wegwitz (middle), Merseburg, Saxony-Anhalt, Germany. Landesmuseum für Vorgeschichte, Halle an der Saale

Pottery of the Bell Beaker culture with zones of fine impressed decoration made with the rims of shells

Among the most impressive monuments of the Neolithic age are the megalithic structures—sanctuaries and burial places built of gigantic stone blocks. Monumental construction of this type spread from the East through the Mediterranean area to the Iberian Peninsula and from there northward up the Atlantic coast to western France and the British Isles. Scandinavia and North Germany seem also to have been touched by it. In England and Ireland especially, megalithic structures continued to be erected well into the Bronze Age. The various regions developed their own types of construction, each of which went through several stages in the course of time. Generally speaking, the evolution begins with an approximately round burial chamber, the entrance to which is of varying length, and ends with huge constructions that must be regarded as monumental funerary halls (cf. pages 76, 77). Inasmuch as some of the stone blocks weigh several tons each, the legend arose that these funerary monuments were built by a race of giants. In most cases, only the ruins of such structures have come down to us, like those which endow several sites on the Lüneburger Heide with a melancholy charm (facing page). But what we see of them today is deceptive, for originally the stones were buried under high earthen mounds which have gradually disappeared over the centuries. Not surprisingly, the decorations in Neolithic tombs refer explicitly to a land or realm of the dead. They occur especially frequently in Brittany, and as far east as Central Germany, but here they consist of cist graves or rude stone slabs sunk into the ground. The tomb at Leuna-Göhlitzsch was built of two long slabs with a narrower slab at either end. Three blocks of stone covered the tomb. The inside walls were partly painted red and covered with incised pictorial representations. The chevron pattern on the slab below seems to suggest a length of fabric made up of four strips sewn together. Over this is traced a bow with loosened string. The triple curvature of this bow would increase the speed of the flying arrow and add force to its impact. To the left can be seen the dead man's quiver, containing a number of arrows, and the strap it hung from.

Megalithic tomb on the Lüneburger Heide, Lower Saxony, Germany

◀ Engraved slab from a cist grave. Stone, length c. 35″. From Leuna-Göhlitzsch, Merseburg, Saxony-Anhalt, Germany. Landesmuseum für Vorgeschichte, Halle an der Saale

La Roche aux Fées. Megalithic passage grave at Essé (Ille-et-Vilaine), France (cf. facing page)

In France, over six thousand megalithic tombs have been discovered, of which more than half are in Brittany. This clearly shows that the route from the Iberian Peninsula to the British Isles ran along the Atlantic coastline. In addition, Brittany is the site of numerous menhirs (upright monoliths) and avenues of huge blocks of stone: these last represent the megalithic conception of sanctuaries (cf. page 80). These types of monumental construction made their appearance early in the third millennium B.C. They thus extend over a time span which, on the basis of other criteria, we may call the Copper Age. The earliest burial structures in France include smaller circular ones with short rectangular antechambers. Here and there, they are built like domes with false vaulting, i.e., with successive courses of stone slabs projecting progressively inward as they approach the apex of the roof. In southwestern England, this type of construction was still in use in the Early Bronze Age to provide burial chambers for an elite class of warriors. The development culminates in the so-called *allées couvertes* (passage graves)—Neolithic tombs with a long tunnel-like entrance. A particularly well-preserved example of these is La Roche aux Fées. It consists of a large antechamber, a low passageway, and a high-ceilinged burial chamber subdivided by four stones placed crosswise. The structure is twenty-four yards long and is composed of forty-one blocks, each of which is estimated to weigh from forty to forty-five tons. The amount of work involved in erecting such a monument presupposes a rigidly organized collective effort. Just what technical devices were used to transport and erect the gigantic stones is not known. In addition to human and animal traction, inclined planes, rollers, and levers (like those used in Mediterranean countries) must have been employed. What we have here is an architecture unconcerned with exterior effects. Conceived of as a shelter, it was concerned only with the interior appearance. Like the hidden tombs of the Pharaohs, its purpose was to preserve the body of the deceased beneath the earth for all time.

La Roche aux Fées. Interior view (cf. facing page)

The photograph shows part of the central structure of the megalithic sanctuary known as Stonehenge. To the right and in the background is the outer circle of trilithons (pairs of upright megaliths with horizontal capstones). To the left are two of the five trilithons arranged in a horseshoe shape around the Altar Stone. The small menhirs between these and the outer ring also formed a circle; while another ring of small stones ran around the central area within the horseshoe arrangement (cf. page 81).

Stonehenge. Megalithic sanctuary on Salisbury Plain, Wiltshire, England

System of menhirs at Ménec, Carnac (Morbihan), France

Unlike the megalithic graves, the architecture of megalithic sanctuaries was meant to be seen from a distance. They served as the scenes of solemn public rituals on a huge scale. At Ménec, 1,169 menhirs, all of them unhewn, are still standing upright on the open moor. Some reach a height of twenty-three feet and several weigh four hundred tons and more. Within a rectangle about three-quarters of a mile long and at least one hundred yards wide, 1,099 blocks are set up in eleven rows. They mark out ten wide avenues, the central one leading up to the open side of a semicircle of seventy stone pillars. Here must have been situated the center of a cult, the nature of which can no longer be determined. The grandiose processional way compelled all participants to move toward the central area. The tremendous size of the complex gives us an idea of the power of the divinity that was worshiped here—perhaps also the power of a priestly caste or a sacred king. Occasionally, individual menhirs possessed a meaning of their own (cf. pages 83, 84). If they are to be interpreted as statues, gigantic imageless sculptures, Celtic legend supplies one clue. According to the legend, an army that had been defeated in battle retreated toward the sea, expecting to escape by ship; but no ships were available and there was no other hope of escape. The warriors decided to make one last stand and were transformed into stones in their exact battle order.

Pytheas, a Greek writer who lived in the middle of the fourth century B.C., mentions a temple dedicated to Apollo on the island of the Hyperboreans. He may have been referring to Stonehenge, for the immense structure could well have been regarded at the time as a Wonder of the World whose fame had spread far beyond the British Isles (see also pages 78–79). The most recent interpretations, according to which this was a Prehistoric observatory, are beside the point. Stonehenge and its architecture must be interpreted in terms of myth, not of astronomical-mathematical computations. Its exact orientation, like that of all sanctuaries, is accounted for by the fact that they were bound up with the cosmic order. At Stonehenge, this orientation is defined by a sacred axis which runs from the so-called Altar Stone at the center, through an opening in the great circle of trilithons and a breach in the wall, along a processional road toward the northeast. At the summer solstice (about June 22), the rays of the rising sun fall on the Altar Stone. This suggests some reference to supernatural powers, but not any elaborate system of sun worship. The structure was begun toward the close of the Neolithic period, but essential parts of it were not finished until the Bronze Age. The monumental circular temple is characteristic of religious beliefs which here found gigantic embodiment in stone and in solemn processions.

Stonehenge. Megalithic sanctuary on Salisbury Plain, Wiltshire, England. Aerial photo from SSE. Bottom right: the so-called Southeast Stone outside the restored outer circle; facing it at the other side of the circle, the Northwest Stone. A processional route (not visible in the photograph) starting from the Altar Stone, on which the rays of the rising sun at the summer solstice fell through openings in the circles of pillars, runs off to the right of the picture. Diameter of the circular earthwork c. 125 yards (cf. pages 78–79)

Nonfigural menhir at Cagliari, Sardinia

Stone steles in schematized human form. From Rocher-des-Domes, Avignon (left), and Lauris (Vaucluse), France. Musée Calvet, Avignon

Isolated menhirs are found in great numbers all over Europe, and are by no means confined to the Neolithic period. What they signified varies considerably according to period and region. Syncretism, i.e., the coalescing of different forms of Prehistoric religion, complicates the task of interpretation. Menhirs, whether they represent gods or the dead, are incontestably related to ritual poles and obelisks, as well as to the earliest steles. In many cases, they can probably be regarded as substitute bodies of a kind. Above all, the so-called menhir statues dating from the Late Neolithic period in western Europe were obviously intended as human figures. In Sardinia, for instance, some stone monuments with breasts are clearly intended as female figures. The little-known menhirs from Corsica are occasionally topped with forms suggesting horned helmets and may well be personifications of warriors. These peculiar statues probably go back to eastern Mediterranean sculptures. In the West, however, they grew progressively less naturalistic and in the end gave way to a rigid geometric

Menhir with schematic female figure in relief. Sandstone, height c. 48″. From Saint-Sernin-sur-Rance (Aveyron), France. Musée Lapidaire de la Société des Lettres, Sciences et Arts à l'Évêché, Rodez

schematism. One intermediate stage in this development
is illustrated by the low relief on stone from Saint-
Sernin-sur-Rance (facing page). Face, breasts, limbs,
and articles of adornment are crudely and clumsily
executed. The shape of the figure is entirely determined
by that of the stone itself. This is why the head seems
to be pulled down between the shoulders and the dis-
proportionate legs seem to hang from the garment. As
a result, all the other proportions are distorted, too.
However, the position of the arms is typical—a posture
delineated also in the clay statuette from Vadastra
dating from approximately the same period (page 67).
Such menhir statues probably represented a goddess of
death and the afterworld, of the same kind that occurs
in megalithic graves in Brittany, and occasionally also
in Germany, in the form of a shield-shaped symbolic
sign with eyes and the suggestion of a nose (cf. also
page 139). Such highly abbreviated signs have their
origins in reliefs like those illustrated on page 83. Their
peculiar charm and effectiveness derive from their basic
geometric form, which rules out all personal expression.
Their very impersonality seems deliberate. The lozenge
ornament on the Lauris relief and the sun symbol on
that from Rocher-des-Domes carry the representation
of faces into an extrapersonal, probably superhuman,
sphere. To the same category belong certain Late Neolithic Iberian gods in which the human figure has been
totally transformed into ornamental design. On the
alabaster cylinder from Estremadura, the eyes are ro-
settes and the arms no more than grooved borders to
the ornamental field.

Cylinder with schematized human face. Alabaster, height $7^7/_8''$.
From a megalithic grave in Estremadura, Spain, exact location
of site unknown. Museo Arqueológico Nacional, Madrid

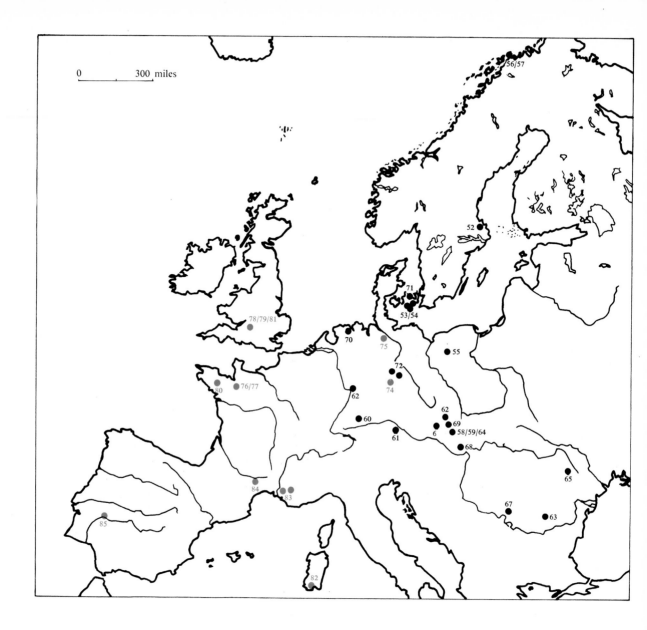

Neolithic sites

Red: menhirs, menhir statues, megalithic constructions.

The time span involved covers a period of almost three thousand years. While the map does not indicate the ultimate origins of this kind of art in Asia Minor, it does suggest Prehistoric lines of communication from there to Sardinia and along the Mediterranean and Atlantic coasts to northern and northeastern Europe. Clay sculptures are the main evidence for no less important lines of communication from Central Europe to the southeast, via the Danube Valley.

Chronological chart of the Neolithic period

The numbers refer to pages. Where the dating is uncertain, a question mark has been added to the page reference. The red shading indicates approximate periods during which individual groups were active.

For the Neolithic period, too, exact dates are hard to arrive at, particularly for the earliest phases. There is not even unanimity as to when the period began. Many writers give the beginning as 3500 B.C. One method of establishing dates is to compare the material cultures of various groups and to find connections between them and advanced Mediterranean civilizations that had historical traditions while most of Europe was still at the Prehistoric stage. However, this method is unsatisfactory and its results are often inaccurate. As for dating by the radioactive carbon (C 14) method, this is still in the early stages of development, but will surely be of considerable use once the technique is sufficiently refined. At present, the margin of error is still very great; for instance, the date obtained for Stonehenge I is 1961 B.C. plus or minus 275 years. The order of succession of particular groups is to some extent clear, but the chart below is far from exhaustive, being restricted to the illustrations in this book. The customary names for the Neolithic peoples derive from their characteristic pottery (e.g., the Bell Beaker culture) or from type sites (e.g., Cucuteni). The diagonal line demarcating possession or nonpossession of copper artifacts emphasizes the economic backwardness of the North, where Mesolithic ways of life survived much longer than elsewhere.

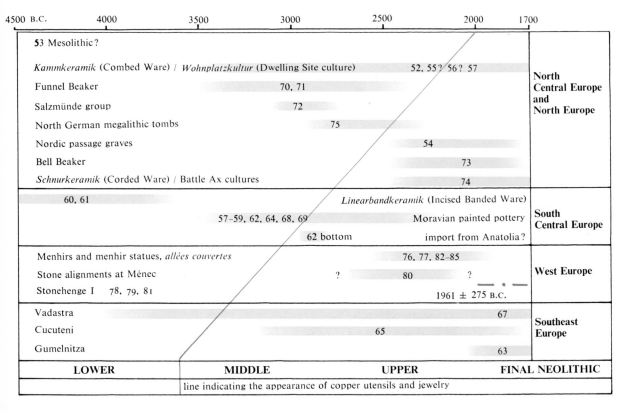

Chart columns: 4500 B.C. — 4000 — 3500 — 3000 — 2500 — 2000 — 1700

North Central Europe and North Europe
- 53 Mesolithic?
- *Kammkeramik* (Combed Ware) / *Wohnplatzkultur* (Dwelling Site culture) — 52, 55? 56? 57
- Funnel Beaker — 70, 71
- Salzmünde group — 72
- North German megalithic tombs — 75
- Nordic passage graves — 54
- Bell Beaker — 73
- *Schnurkeramik* (Corded Ware) / Battle Ax cultures — 74

South Central Europe
- 60, 61
- 57–59, 62, 64, 68, 69
- 62 bottom
- *Linearbandkeramik* (Incised Banded Ware)
- Moravian painted pottery
- import from Anatolia?

West Europe
- Menhirs and menhir statues, *allées couvertes* — 76, 77, 82–85
- Stone alignments at Ménec — ? 80 ?
- Stonehenge I — 78, 79, 81 — 1961 ± 275 B.C.

Southeast Europe
- Vadastra — 67
- Cucuteni — 65
- Gumelnitza — 63

LOWER | MIDDLE | UPPER | FINAL NEOLITHIC

line indicating the appearance of copper utensils and jewelry

FROM THE BRONZE AGE TO THE EARLY IRON AGE

The period beginning sometime between 1800 and 1700 and ending approximately 500 B.C. has been variously subdivided, largely on the basis of types of material culture. In North Central Europe and Scandinavia, the time span discussed here includes several periods or stages of the Bronze Age and the earliest phase of the Iron Age. In South Central Europe and the regions adjoining it, the successive periods are currently designated (partly on the basis of other criteria) as Bronze Age, Urn Field, and Hallstatt. The same division is used for the rest of Europe, but regional peculiarities are usually emphasized by additional designations. We cannot go into details here. The period as a whole comprises a number of stages of development, both cultural and technological (see pages 156, 157).

Economic life in the Bronze Age was based on agriculture and animal husbandry. Mining and the smelting of ore, however, require specialists, and soon gave rise to a separate class of craftsmen. As the demand for metal increased, new stylistic areas arose, as well as a new social stratification. This was also partly an expression of the varied stakes in ownership of the means of production. Some regions were ruled by a warrior caste, a kind of military aristocracy, who took to their graves with them emblems of their worldly power to serve as proof of their earthly dignity in the afterworld. From the outset, goldsmiths—who made their appearance at an early date, at the same time as the blacksmiths—worked for this class of warriors. Parade weapons decorated with gold, like the mace from Clandon Barrow, are emblems of the power wielded by an archaic

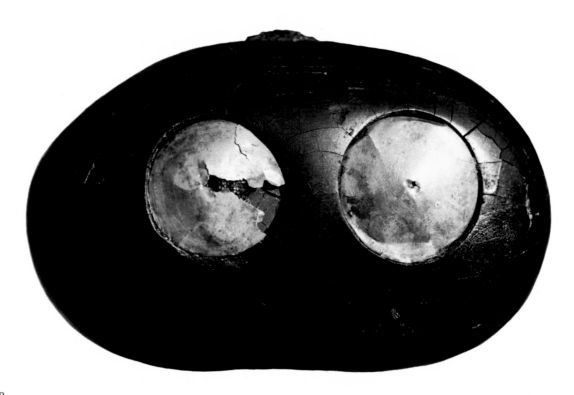

Embossed plaque. Sheet gold, length 5⁷/₈″. From Clandon Barrow, Dorset, England. Museum, Dorchester

ruling class which had gained control over all wealth. Two gold cups, similar in shape and manufacture, one from Rillaton in Wessex and the other from Fritzdorf, near Bonn (page 91), point to contacts with the Aegean civilization: both are probably imitations of Mycenaean vessels in precious metal and testify to the continued existence of maritime trade between the eastern Mediterranean and the British Isles, just as in megalithic times. In the later phases of the Bronze Age, Irish goldwork was conspicuous.

◀ Mace. Black lignite or slate with gold knobs, diameter c. 3″.
From Clandon Barrow, Dorset, England. Museum, Dorchester

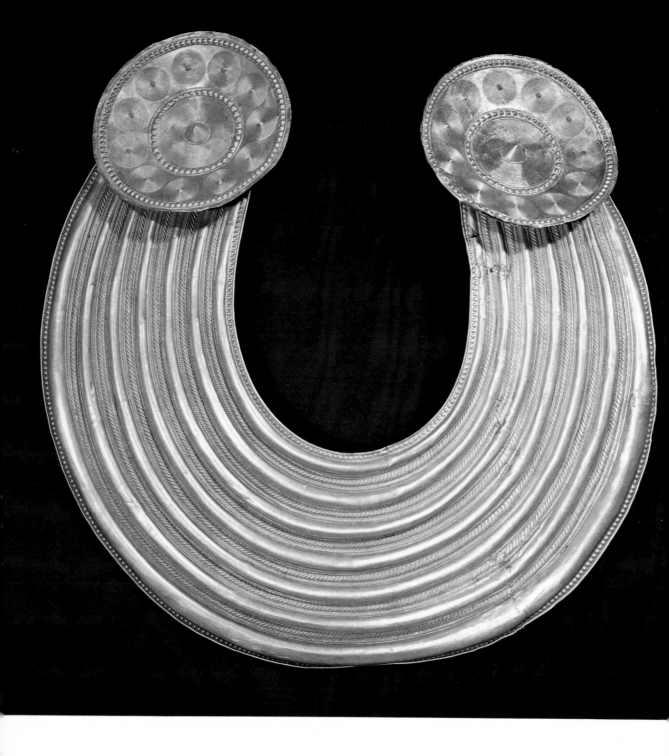

Collar. Embossed repoussé sheet gold, greatest diameter 12″. From
Gleninsheen, County Clare, Ireland. National Museum, Dublin

The collar from Gleninsheen (facing page) is merely one of hundreds of gold objects of personal ornament which were buried in the moor. Other evidence at the site shows that they were never intended to be disinterred. Most such objects seem to have been dropped into lakes and streams (which have silted up in the course of time) to serve as adornments in the afterworld. On the other hand, many ritual objects seem to have been buried to prevent them from being stolen or desecrated. The latter include the so-called solar disks, like the one from Moordorf (page 93), which must have served a ritual purpose similar to the gold disk on the Trundholm wagon (cf. page 121). The gold headpiece from Schifferstadt (page 92) was surely used for some ritual purpose, too. The richly embossed tracery represents a very rare category of finds, the first high point of an indigenous art of metalwork.

Cup. Wrought sheet gold, height 4³/₄″. From Fritzdorf, Bonn, North-Rhine Westphalia, Germany. Rheinisches Landesmuseum, Bonn

So-called *Solar Disk*. Embossed sheet gold, diameter 5³/₄″. From Moordorf, Aurich, Lower Saxony, Germany. Niedersächsisches Landesmuseum, Hanover

◀ Conical headpiece, the so-called *Golden Hat of Schifferstadt*. Embossed wrought sheet gold, height 11¹/₈″. From a hoard discovered at Schifferstadt, Speyer, Rhineland-Palatinate, Germany. Historisches Museum der Pfalz, Speyer

Bronze articles of personal adornment. Belt box with bosses, diameter c. 7″; spiral wire bracelet, height c. 2¹/₄″; cast torque, diameter c. 8″; and spiral hair pin, length c. 9″. Found together at Røgerup, Zealand, Denmark. Nationalmuseet, Copenhagen

Amphora and cups with long handles terminating in stylized horses' heads. Amphora of sheet bronze, height 13¹/₄″; cups (found inside the amphora) of embossed gold, diameter c. 4³/₄″. From Mariesminde Mose, Fyn, Denmark. Nationalmuseet, Copenhagen

Vessel stand. Embossed sheet bronze with attached rings, height 12³/₄″. Four small three-dimensional birds surround the lozenge-shaped opening in each of the vertical connecting braces. From Hallstatt, grave 507, Upper Austria. Naturhistorisches Museum, Vienna

A complete dependence on the importation of bronze and copper did not hinder northern Europe from developing outstanding techniques in the working of metals, or from forming individual stylistic areas. The bronze jewelry from Denmark (page 94) belongs to a period in which the early spiral ornament was being gradually broken down. The torque with its sharp-cut molding, providing a most effective contrast between areas of light and dark, is characteristic of the liveliness of Nordic ornamental art. Finished bronze articles were, of course, also imported, together with the raw material. The large vessel from Mariesminde Mose (page 95) probably comes from southeast Central Europe, as is evidenced by the embossed decoration of boats, birds, and sun. The gold cups, on the other hand, are local products. The stylized horses' heads which grow organically out of the long handles demonstrate a successful adaptation of decorative and figural forms to the shape of the object. By contrast, the birds on the bronze stand from Hallstatt impress one as being afterthoughts, even though the bird motif is repeated, together with the sun wheel, in the embossed patterns.

Utensils found in a horseman's grave. Amphora, bronze, 13³/₈″; two dishes, bronze, diameter 9¹/₂″; cup, dark-red painted pottery, height 2¹/₂″. From Grosseibstadt, Königshofen im Grabfeld, Bavaria, Germany. Prähistorische Staatssammlung, Munich

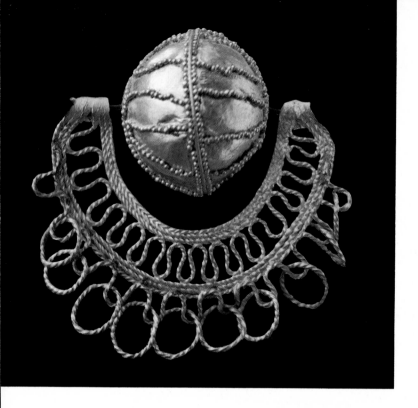

Pendant of sheet gold and gold wire. The hollow ball consists of two semispheres of wrought gold soldered together and decorated in granulation technique. The ball revolves around an axis, which also supports a network of "plaited" wires soldered together into a loop design. Attached to the border are free-moving tiny gold rings. Over-all height c. 1″. From Jegenstorf, Canton of Bern, Switzerland. Historisches Museum, Bern

Neck ring with loop-and-button clasp. Embossed sheet gold, inside diameter c. 6″, weight c. 4 oz. From Uttendorf, Braunau, Upper Austria. Oberösterreichisches Landesmuseum Francisco-Carolinum, Linz

Conoid vessel with everted lip. Graphite painting and incised and impressed ornamentation, height 10¹/₄″, greatest diameter 14⁵/₈″. From Wilsingen, Münsingen, Baden-Württemberg, Germany. Württembergisches Landesmuseum, Stuttgart

Toward the close of the Hallstatt epoch, trade between the South and the North increased considerably, as is attested particularly by finds in northern Switzerland, eastern France, and southwestern Germany—areas that are notable for their royal graves. Here, groups seem to have existed that were sufficiently sophisticated to carry on systematic trade with the South, above all with the Greek colony at Massilia (present-day Marseilles). From the part of Italy colonized by the Greeks, known as Magna Graecia, came wine jars and drinking goblets for use in the courts of rulers great and small. Italic utensils of bronze and clay were also imported; the little grooved cup from the Grosseibstadt burial, for example, came originally from the Este culture in northern Italy (page 96). Along with these, Etruscan articles have been found, such as the miniature gold pendant from Jegenstorf, a goldsmith's masterpiece. The craftsmen of the most advanced communities north of the Alps were scarcely inferior to the Greek and Italic ones, at least in the working of gold. Among other examples which might be cited are neck rings, such as that from Uttendorf (facing page), which served at once for personal adornment and as badges of rank (cf. page 135). The embossing was done with differently shaped bronze punches. These works are characterized by the stereotyped repetition, the articulation into decorative zones, and the lack of undecorated surfaces.

Pottery, which now, for the first time, achieved the rank of a specialized craft, is decorated in a similar way. Apparently, it was no longer a home industry but was made in workshops by skilled craftsmen. The potter's wheel was still unknown, but a primitive turntable was already in use for shaping the lower part of very large vessels. The graves contain storage jars, ladles, dishes, bowls, basins of all shapes and sizes, occasionally other furnishings as well. This is in keeping with the way the burial chambers are arranged, often resembling living quarters, not infrequently in the shape of a cabin or small house. Painting, graphite coating, chip carving, impressed patterns, and incrustation are often combined on pottery vessels. The articulation of the outer surface into smooth zones and patterned zones invariably follows a geometric schema. The painterly effects

Shiny black pottery jug with incised geometric decoration, originally filled in with white pigment (the white filling is restored). Height 7$^{1}/_{8}$". From Beilngries, Bavaria, Germany. Prähistorische Staatssammlung, Munich

Ladle with hooked handle in the shape of an animal head. Diameter 3⁷/₈″. From Oberwiesenacker, Parsberg, Bavaria, Germany. Museum für Vor- und Frühgeschichte, Berlin

Painted vessel. Clay, height 3⁷/₈″. From Fischbach, Burglengenfeld, Bavaria, Germany. Prähistorische Staatssammlung,
Munich

Pottery bowl, stepped in cross section, with incised and impressed decoration. Diameter 13³/₄". From Tannheim, Biberach an der Riss, Baden-Württemberg, Germany. Württembergisches Landesmuseum, Stuttgart

are particularly striking where the smooth surfaces like that on the vessel from Wilsingen (page 99) are covered with a coat of graphite and the separate decorative fields have varying incised or impressed patterns. Sometimes the ornamentation is filled in with white pigment, so that it stands out against the darker ground (page 100). The pattern always emphasizes the form of the vessel and, similarly, decorations on the insides of bowls are always concentric in design (see above and page 104). The same concentric layout, in which the decorative pattern is often distributed over the body of the vessel in groups of three, also occurs in painted decorations. Thus, the double chevron band on the red jar from Fischbach (page 101) joins up with two other similar patterns to form, on the base of the vessel, a triskelion design.

Painted decorations often seem to include symbolic signs. The coloring itself depends, among other things, on the given type of clay. Thus, red is obtained by adding iron oxide to a diluted clay solution. A cream-colored coating is a slip which takes on its light color during firing. Painted ladles from among drinking utensils are sometimes modeled after bronze vessels: the handle in the shape of a stylized animal on the oval ladle from Oberwiesenacker (page 101) is an example. Some ornamental motifs are widely distributed, while others are found in a single area only, or are only made in a limited number of colors there. This is most likely accounted for by the existence of local workshops with their special skills and clientele.

Painted high-necked vessel of the Alb-Salem type. Height 8⅝". From Burrenhof, Erkenbrechtsweiler, Nürtingen, Baden-Württemberg, Germany. Württembergisches Landesmuseum, Stuttgart

Painted pottery bowl of the Alb-Salem type, stepped in cross section, with incised and impressed decoration. Diameter $21^5/_8''$. From Sternberg, Münsingen, Baden-Württemberg, Germany. Württembergisches Landesmuseum, Stuttgart

Only a few pictorial representations have come down to us from the Bronze Age proper. Not until the Urn Field period, and then even more in the Hallstatt, do animal and human representations become more frequent. These include pottery vessels in the shape of animals, whose function is often uncertain. The small vessel from Hrubčice (facing page) has what seems to be a stylized bull's head. This may have served as a spout to be drunk from, or the vessel may have been a crudely executed rhyton for pouring out a consecrated liquid (cf. page 119). The painted bowl from Donnerskirchen with three spouts shaped like bulls' heads probably belongs in the same category (page 109).

The finest of the animal figures are small bronze sculptures, although technical problems sometimes obtrude upon formal excellence. The peculiarly arched necks of the two figures from Vestby (page 106), for instance, could hardly have been intended, and certainly are not typical of the animal species represented. The method of casting accounts for the peculiarity. X-ray photographs show that a separate cast was made of the head (with neck and horns), which was then stuck into a clumsy wax model of the body. This model, with its iron core, was coated with clay and then cast in bronze. As for the bronze vessel from Hallstatt (page 107), the technique employed led to an otherwise peculiar result. Both the form and the decoration here are borrowings from Early Geometric Greek bowls, the lids of which were usually topped with statuettes of horses. On the Hallstatt vessel, however, we find a cow and a calf, the only difference between them being their relative size; their differing proportions were ignored. However, since there was no lid, the craftsman used his cow to serve

Animal-shaped pottery vessel. Height 5$^1/_8$". From Hrubčice, Prostějov, Czechoslovakia. Museum, Olomouc

Animal figurines. Bronze over an iron core, length $4^5/_8''$ and $4^7/_8''$. From Vestby, Akershus, Norway. Universitetets Oldsaksamling, Oslo

Caldron with handle in the form of a cow and calf. Bronze, diameter 11³/₄″, length of cow 5⁵/₈″. From Hallstatt, grave 671, Upper Austria. Naturhistorisches Museum, Vienna

as a handle, jutting in from the rim and riveted to the floor of the vessel by means of a brace. The bowl or caldron and its figurative decoration are, in consequence, entirely unrelated. They are in marked contrast to the elegant way in which, for example, the stylized horses' heads on the gold cups from Mariesminde Mose (page 95) seem to grow out of the handles. Even the bulls' heads on the pottery vessel from Donnerskirchen (page 109) are more successful on this score. Compact and reduced to essential features, they are beautiful, as well as functional, parts of the whole.

For all that, Prehistoric art can hardly be compared with contemporary small sculpture in Greece and Italy. Although based on the same geometric forms, its development toward schematization and stylization reflects

Bull. Cast bronze, height c. 3″. From the Býčí Skála cave, Adamov, Moravia, Czechoslovakia. (The little sculpture was inside a bronze vessel containing burned millet.) Naturhistorisches Museum, Vienna

technical inferiority. It never goes consciously beyond the schema to achieve a style governed by well-defined rules. Many animal figures are devoid of artistic intentions, the makers having merely brought out certain features of their subjects without creating any aesthetic balance. Thus, because the little bronze bull from Hallstatt stands on legs like stumps of wood, the image produced is a distorted one (page 110). The only features of a bull regarded as important enough to delineate with some care were the horns, the dewlap, and the sexual parts. By contrast, the bull from Býčí Skála (facing page)—a site which has yielded remarkable finds and which was apparently a place of sacrifice—is one of the rare Prehistoric works that, despite distorted proportions, suggest a truly artistic approach. Although the forms are simplified, they have by no means been ignored. Apparently, the artist was less interested in particular detail than in bringing out a bull's essential characteristics: the powerful, commanding head, massive forequarters, and the firm-as-a-rock way the animal carries its weight on its legs.

Painted vessel with three spouts in the shape of schematized bulls' heads. Clay, height c. 11³/₄″. From Donnerskirchen, Burgenland, Austria. Museum, Eisenstadt

The Hallstatt period derives its name from a large cemetery near Hallstatt in the Salzkammergut district of Austria. Hundreds of graves in this area have yielded an impressive number of artifacts. This little bronze bull and the vessel stand shown on page 97 were found here in a grave together with resplendent jewelry and a sword with an ivory hilt inlaid with amber. The site indicates that a prosperous community existed here, its prosperity perhaps derived from salt mines and lively trade. The fibula from grave 94 (facing page) gives some idea of the comparative luxury that was enjoyed at Hallstatt. The fibulae, or ornamental brooches, are sometimes quite large, especially when they were intended to be worn by women. Something very like "barbaric splendor" is occasionally encountered: anklets, bracelets, and necklaces sometimes weigh several pounds. The fibula from Hallstatt has a catch on the same principle as the modern safety pin. This particular fastening dates from a late phase of the Hallstatt epoch, and is found in some numbers with attached clappers. What is uncommon, however, is to find two little figures of horses on the catchplate, as in this example. Like the little

birds on the vessel stand, their function is purely decorative; the craftsman did not even try to relate them to the fibula's function or to the clappers suspended from it. If we assume that the clappers and the schematic horse decorations served some magical purpose or intention, then their juxtaposition might seem less arbitrary. However, in this and other such works, it appears that motifs were piled on motifs for no other reason than the gratification of a primitive delight in conspicuous wealth.

Schematized bull. Cast bronze, length 4″. From Hallstatt, grave 507, Upper Austria. Naturhistorisches Museum, Vienna

Fibula with schematized horses on the catchplate and pendant clappers. Bronze, width of fibula c. 6″, over-all length c. 13″. From Hallstatt, grave 94, Upper Austria. Oberösterreichisches Landesmuseum Francisco-Carolinum, Linz

Rattle in the shape of a bird with pebbles inside. Clappers were attached to the holes in the neck. Clay, height $4^3/_8$″. From Degerndorf, Parsberg, Bavaria, Germany. Prähistorische Staatssammlung, Munich

Bird-shaped and pig-shaped clay rattles with pebbles inside, from Switzerland. Bird, length 6″, from Zurich; left-hand piglet, length $3^3/_8$″, from Auvernier, Canton of Neuchâtel; right-hand piglet, length 4″, from Corcelettes, Canton of Waadt. Schweizerisches Landesmuseum, Zurich

Since so many rattles of such different kinds date from it, the Hallstatt period inevitably takes on an almost shamanistic flavor. Clay birds with pebbles inside and occasionally holes at the neck for attaching clappers seem to have been used in magic rituals by priests or witch doctors (facing page). Small figures of other animals, such as the piglets from Auvernier and Corcelettes, were less often used for this purpose. Representations of birds also appear in conjunction with solar and boat symbols. The boat with the sun-disk at the center and birds' heads at bow and stern is regarded by specialists as the most prominent ritual image of the Urn Field culture in South Central and southeastern Europe (cf. the embossed design on the bronze amphora illustrated on page 95). In the bronze pendant rattle from Kirchenreinbach, the boat (at the top) is still recognizable, but the solar disk has been replaced by four loops which had the practical purpose of serving as the means of suspending the rattle. Whether the symbolic boat still retains its old meaning here is uncertain. Originally, it must have been conceived as a mythical union of boat and sun, the eternal alternation of night and day viewed as travel in time, the bird denoting either a deity or a divine creature. A combination of symbols so heavy with possible meanings could doubtless be adequately expressed only through schematic representation.

Rattle with appendages. Bronze, outside diameter of the ring 3³/₄″. From Kirchenreinbach, Sulzbach-Rosenberg, Bavaria, Germany. Collection of the Naturhistorische Gesellschaft, Nuremberg

Images of horses appear once more in the Hallstatt period, but now they are geometrically schematized. Nevertheless, the classical prototype is still occasionally recognizable. The four little clay horses from Zainingen were without doubt modeled on Greek originals. This is apparent from the exaggeratedly long, gently rounded necks and the tiny heads. What is certain is that they embody the same principle as Greek statuettes of horses of the Geometric style. Yet the group shows clearly that the artist's intention was primarily symbolic, not artistic. This much at least can be inferred from the pairing of males and females. Keeping this in mind, we ought to consider the figures on the golden bowl from Zürich-Altstetten (facing page) solely in terms of their symbolic meaning. Obviously, the horse shown here with the sun and the moon has some cosmogonic significance, perhaps of the same kind as the solar wagon from Trundholm (page 121). Moreover, the golden bowl exemplifies a tendency peculiar to works from the Late Hallstatt and La Tène periods, namely, the tendency to reverse the roles of background and decoration. In the work shown here, the representations of sun, moon, and animals are reserved as smooth surfaces, while small bosses are punched all over the body of the

Two male and two female horses. Clay, height 5¹/₄" and 4¹/₂". From a burial mound at Zainingen, Münsingen, Baden-Württemberg, Germany. Württembergisches Landesmuseum, Stuttgart

Bowl with embossed decoration in which sun, moon, and animal motifs are reserved. Gold, diameter 9⁷/₈″. From Zürich-Altstetten, Switzerland. Schweizerisches Landesmuseum, Zurich

bowl. This technique is basically no more than a variation of the play with ornament which had its simple predecessors in the Neolithic rapport patterns (page 73) and reached its brilliant climax in the goldwork of the La Tène period (page 199). Such a daring handling of formal elements always reflects a Prehistoric or an anticlassical conception of art.

All the same, Prehistoric craftsmanship goes back again and again to Mediterranean prototypes. Of course, it is handicapped by its still primitive techniques. The three figures at the top of the clay pot from Fischbach (page 116) in their extreme linear schematization would not be recognized as human, had we not unmistakable, much more legible drawings which show that even these ultimately go back to the more artistically stylized friezes of figures on Attic pottery (cf. fig. 11). The lines on the pot from Fischbach are all made with the help of what is called a "roulette," i.e., a toothed wheel that makes little incised dots when moved over a suitable surface. It is a tool with which it is almost impossible to draw a curved line. This roulette technique explains why men riding horses around the bottom of the pot are suggested by straight lines only. To repeat,

Pot with schematized human and animal figures in roulette technique. Clay, height 9⁷/₈″. From Fischbach, Burglengenfeld, Bavaria, Germany. Prähistorische Staatssammlung, Munich

what the design was intended to depict can be made clear only by comparison with more easily interpreted representations (cf. pages 180, 181). Small sculpture always shows the true riding position, as in the horse fibula from Este (facing page). In Frög, horses and riders were found together with other statuettes whose gestures are clearly those of mourning, prayer, or ceremonial giving of the hands at a funeral. These lead figures thus also throw some light on the pictorial scenes of Fischbach as funeral celebrations with a procession of horsemen or wagons (cf. page 122), a motif which made its first appearance in Greek Geometric vase painting (cf. fig. 11).

Standing and riding figures, originally fixed to pottery vessels. Cast lead, length of horses c. 2½". From burial mounds at Frög, Rosegg, Carinthia, Austria. Landesmuseum für Kärnten, Klagenfurt

Fibula with schematized figures of men on horseback. Bronze, length 2". From Este, Veneto, Italy. Museo Civico, Este

At every stage in the Age of Metals, Italy kept up trade contacts with the North. These were especially close in the sixth century B.C., when the Etruscans were flourishing politically and economically. From the fifth century on, large areas of Italy came under Roman rule. Thus ended the Prehistoric epoch in this part of Europe, and in the centuries that followed, Italian culture can no longer be measured by the standards obtaining in the rest of Europe. At first, Italy was primarily influenced by the advanced eastern Mediterranean civilizations, but the artistic stimuli supplied by the latter gave rise to distinctive Italian forms. Italy, in turn, disseminated these stimuli northward and handed on many technical devices that influenced Europe's Prehistoric art. Among the innovations were the lathe, the turntable, and even so complex a technique as the manufacture of colored glass products. It is noteworthy that yellow and blue predominate in the glass beads of the La Tène period, just as in the glass fibula from Villanova, which goes back to the Urn Field period. In the askos from Benacci (facing page), the ancient Mediterranean bull motif and the Hallstatt horseman figure are combined in a rather arbitrary manner. But the Italic potter, who apparently worked to close specifications, must have been aware of the incongruity, for he made an effort to combine the two figures into a homogeneous decoration. He also made sensitive use of embossed and roulette ornamentation to give a seemingly organic structure to the vessel. In this, he went a step further than potters north of the Alps, most of whom laid emphasis on the way the object was broken up into different zones of decoration.

Animal-shaped askos with handle in the form of a man on horseback. Clay, length c. 8″. From Benacci, Bologna, Italy. Museo Civico, Bologna

◀ Fibula. Bronze and colored glass. Length 3⅞″. From Villanova, Bologna, Italy. Museo Civico, Bologna

Horse, probably originally harnessed to a solar wagon. Bronze with inlaid amber eyes, length c. 7″. From Tågaborgshöjden, Hälsingborg, Skåne, Sweden. Statens Historiska Museum, Stockholm

Horse. Bronze, height 3¹/₂″. From Obřany, Brno, Czechoslovakia. Moravian Museum, Brno

The Solar Wagon of Trundholm. Chassis, horse, and disk are cast in bronze; the disk is made up of two convex halves held together by an encircling ring; a solar disk of wrought sheet gold is superposed on either side; the horse's head, neck, and chest have been given an ornamental treatment similar to that found on the solar disk, and the shaft of the vehicle is also decorated; over-all length 23⅝″. From a bog at Trundholm, Zealand, Denmark. Nationalmuseet, Copenhagen

Not until the Age of Metals did horses, horsemanship, and wagons begin to assume historical and cultural importance in Europe. The four-wheeled cart seems to have been the earliest vehicle. The tiny equipage from Frög, however, with its four-wheeled wagon drawn by six pairs of horses, certainly does not represent an ordinary vehicle. It is probably related to the ritual carriage from Strettweg, which is unmistakably characterized by a scene of sacrifice and a bowl (page 147). In the North, where the symbolic combination of sun and horse was current, horses drawing solar disks on wheels appear much as we might expect (page 121). The miniature models give us some idea of the solemn processions that must have been a feature of religious festivities. Probably most of the little bronze horses that have come down to us were originally pulling such carriages. For all their crudeness, they occasionally reveal the special character of their function by some little peculiarity such as inlaid amber eyes (page 120).

Miniature wagon with six pairs of horses. Lead, length of carriage with shaft 11⅜″. From a burial mound at Frög, Rosegg, Carinthia, Austria. Landesmuseum für Kärnten, Klagenfurt

▲

Two-wheeled war chariot with horses. Height 27⅝″. Detail of a rock drawing at Frännarp, Gryt, Skåne, Sweden

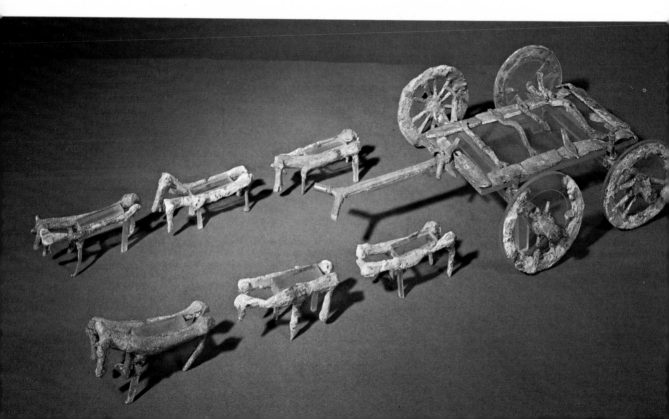

The two-wheeled chariot drawn by a team of horses always served warlike purposes (cf. page 155). Archaeologically, it is possible to trace the type back as far as the Late Hallstatt and the Early La Tène periods. The Swedish rock drawings at Frännarp (facing page) can be assigned, though only just, to the same epoch. In these drawings, horses and vehicle are still constructed in the old abstract way; i.e., they are broken down into their most striking elements. The body of the chariot is shown from above, the two wheels as though lying flat on the ground. Similarly, the horses seem to be lying prone on either side of the shaft. The chariot represented in the stone-lined grave at Kivik (pages 132–33) is similarly recognizable by the placing of two wheels next to each other. Here, however, the horses and the charioteer, at least, appear in lateral view, as they were already represented in the more advanced Mediterranean civilizations, e.g., in the battle scene relief on this funerary stele from Mycenae. But profile views of this kind do not appear in the North until a fairly late date. The drawing at Kivik is an exception. Like the Mycenaean relief, it dates from the Early Bronze Age and is thus far older than the Frännarp drawings. This circumstance can be accounted for only by Bronze Age contacts with the eastern Mediterranean region maintained via the Iberian-Atlantic sea route since megalithic times, but apparently broken off later.

Low relief with spiral decoration and battle scene between a foot soldier and a man in a chariot. Stone funerary stele from shaft grave V at Mycenae, Greece. National Museum, Athens

Two-handled finial, probably representing a bird mask. Bronze, height c. 2³/₄″. From Glasbacka, Ljungby, Halland, Sweden. Statens Historiska Museum, Stockholm

The Nordic rock drawings from the Bronze Age are not remarkable for their artistic qualities, nor do they convey any very clear information. In most cases, they have to be studied in conjunction with other categories of finds, and even then it is often impossible to determine whether they represent mythical events or ritual enactments of such events. In every case, we are dealing with pictorial styles whose purpose is to identify specific figures and their actions. The rock drawings give us some idea of how those oldest of the arts, the dance and mime, were practiced in Prehistoric times. Governed by strict rules and hallowed traditions, the performers had little room for free invention, and the draftsman who recorded the performances was similarly subjected to strict rules. On the rock drawing at Kallsängen (facing page), the dancers appear to be costumed as birds with wings, tails, and beaks. The use of such animal costumes is not uncommon for the ritual dance or procession and may have been related to the transmission of bird symbolism from Central

◄ Dancing human figures in bird costumes. Rock drawing. Kallsängen, Bottna, Bohuslän, Sweden

Ritual dancer in ceremonial costume (?). Detail from a rock drawing, height of figure 35³/₈″. Järrestad, Skåne, Sweden

Europe to the North. Northern finds in this category, however, are executed quite capriciously. The little finial from Glasbacka (page 125) probably reproduces a bird mask of the kind used in ceremonial dances at Kallsängen. Here, natural forms are disregarded, the main emphasis being given to the beak—a stylization possible and credible only in a mask.

The male dancer in a rock drawing at Järrestad, too, seems to be wearing a costume with a tail. Here, we are at once struck by the eloquence of the arms and hands, and the peculiar position of the legs. It would be a mistake to attribute the ungainliness to some lack of skill in the draftsman, to some graphic accident, so to speak. That the attitude depicted here had a definite ritual meaning is proved by the fact that a great many sacred or funerary figures are shown in a similar pose. The outstretched thumbs on the stele from Hirschlanden (page 135) and in the

little ritual statuette from Denmark (page 140) are also found elsewhere. The slightly bent knees of the standing wooden figures in the boat from Roos Carr (page 149) are seen in the little bronze male figures from Stockhult (page 138). Such repetitions suggest that figural representation was subject to strict rules. Even on razor handles, certain motifs and no others appear, perhaps because razors often served ritual purposes in much the same way as needles used in tattooing. The way in which the human figure on the handle from Simris holds his arms can hardly be described as ornamental or functional: the gesture has some precise significance, though just what it is, is hard to say (cf. page 140). Moreover, the headdress of the figure is related to the horned cap worn by the male figure from Järrestad (facing page); and finally, the tail of the animal costume of the Järrestad dancer is stylized as a loop in the Simris figure.

Razor handle (front and side views). Bronze, length c. $2^3/_4''$. From Simris, Skåne, Sweden. Statens Historiska Museum, Stockholm

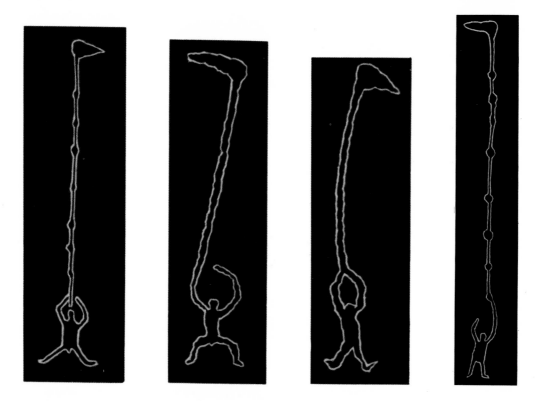

Independently of time and place, primitive peoples at the same stage of development exhibit very similar types of pictorial and symbolic representation. This affinity for the same or similar motifs rests upon common modes of behavior; where pictorial evidence is lacking, the affinity can be inferred from archaeological finds. In this connection, weapons—especially oversized weapons—are most instructive. That they are depicted or used for ritual purposes in preference to other implements can be explained both historically and psychologically. The sword, for instance, was a symbol of justice as late as the Middle Ages. The oldest weapons, however, are the spear, the dagger, and the ax. Accordingly, they occupy the most prominent place in the ritual picture. In Ligurian rock drawings, we see men carrying a kind of halberd which seems to be enormously long. Similarly, the axes brandished by male figures in a Nordic boat (page 148) look gigantic. But the pictorial exaggeration is based on reality, for the pictures refer to huge weapons too unwieldy to be of practical use. They are often richly decorated and occasionally inlaid with gold. All of them come from treasure depositories and were therefore generally public religious property. Conditions of ownership are no longer as clear-cut when, with the beginning of the Urn Field epoch, the bronze equipment was also used by the ruling class as insignia. As such, the weapons go back to Mediterranean prototypes. The bronze shields, for example, from Central, western, and northeastern Europe could not possibly have been of any use in actual battles, for one blow of a sword would have split them in two. Probably they were intended as ceremonial weapons, as is suggested by the great amount of labor that went into making them, and even more by the character of the sites where they have been found. They were mostly buried in bogs or dropped into lakes or streams, apparently as sacrificial offerings. Iberian and southern French shields are known to us only from drawings. One funerary stele from Solana de Cabañas shows the figure of the deceased with his spear, his shield, and a four-wheeled chariot (page 130). This West European type of shield is represented in the rest of Europe by only one

Men carrying outsize ceremonial weapons. Ligurian rock drawing, height of the right-hand figure c. 20″, of the others c. 10–11″. Val Fontanalba, Italy

Axhead and spear point, ceremonial weapons from a treasure depository. Bronze, length 10¹/₄″ and 13³/₈″. From Krottenthal, Dingolfing, Bavaria, Germany. Prähistorische Staatssammlung, Munich

example, a rock drawing in Ireland (page 130). Apparently, in the West, intercourse between neighbors along the Atlantic shore was comparable to the close contacts maintained by groups in the Danube Valley, for example. Here, too, the cult of the dead reflects this most clearly. The bronze votive hands and mask from Kleinklein in Styria (page 131) are matched by similar gold pieces found, among other places, at Trebenište in Macedonia. In both instances, hands and masks were found in graves of prominent warriors, and their weapons are nearly identical. This class of warrior set the political standards and preserved a tradition of mythical thought that had originated in Greece's heroic age. Indeed, the gold masks from Mycenae, typologically speaking, supply the original forms of the Central European bronze masks. Though artistically insignificant, the latter vividly illustrate a desire to preserve the image of the deceased that is perfectly in keeping with the classical mentality. The same desire is expressed in a more general form elsewhere, in stylized drawings (page 130), face urns, and funerary steles (page 135).

Funerary stele with figure of the deceased and his weapons: spear and sword (top); below these, his shield; and below that, his chariot. The two objects shown between the shield and the human figure are unidentified. Height 51″. From Solana de Cabañas, Logrosán, Cáceres, Spain. Museo Arqueológico Nacional, Madrid

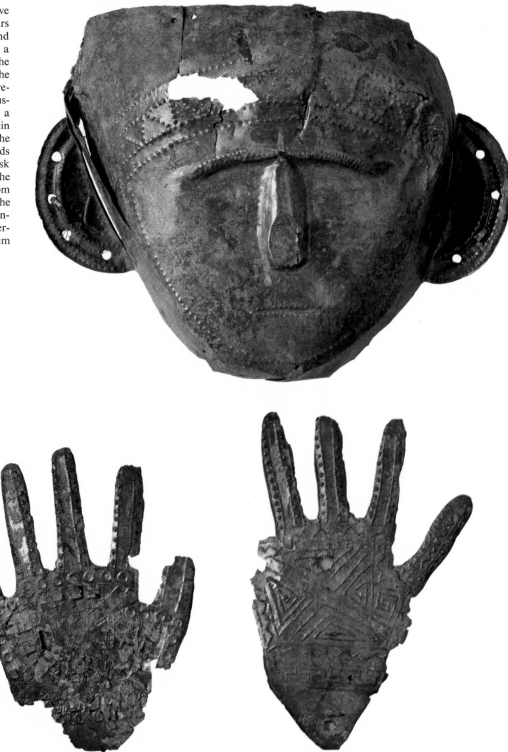

Death mask and votive hands. The semicircular ears are riveted to the mask and were in turn nailed to a wooden container for the ashes of the deceased. The embossed decoration represents features of burial custom: a headband with a chevron pattern and a chin strap. Bronze, width of the mask 9″; length of the hands 5¹/₂″ and 6¹/₈″. The mask from a royal grave on the Kröllkogel; the hands from another burial site on the Schmiedkogel, near Kleinklein, Styria, Austria. Steiermärkisches Landesmuseum Joanneum, Graz

The Kivik burial chamber (13′7″ × 3′ × 4′) was situated under a high mound. It consisted of four large stone slabs lengthwise and one smaller slab at either end, and was covered by three heavy stone blocks. Seven of the eight slabs that lined it have symbolic signs incised and ritual scenes obviously referring to burial customs. The representations begin on the east wall, continue on the west wall running in the opposite direction, and seem to depict a definite sequence of rites. At the entrance stood a slab (now lost) showing a slender pyramid and ritual axes (fig. 4). The stone with four horses—two above and two below a simple ornamental band (facing page)—was originally part of the east wall. Two of the horses seem to be sacrificed as the ceremony approaches its end, while the other two are harnessed to a chariot (second stone from the left, below) to carry the dead man into the other world, or perhaps to be given in offering to some deity. Below the charioteer, there is a procession of eight men, unmistakably wearing masks. They clearly indicate the sequence of the events depicted, for on the next stone, the last before the entrance on the west wall, they form two groups around an altar or caldron, or some central sacred point (middle frieze on first stone from the left). At the same time, two men blowing *luren* (bronze S-shaped trumpets) signal the conclusion of the solemn ceremony. Some of the signs and figures are undecipherable.

West wall of the stone cist grave from Kivik, Skåne, Sweden. Statens Historiska Museum, Stockholm

Decorated slabs from the Kivik cist grave. Left: stone no. 3 from the east wall, showing two horses above and two below a purely ornamental zone. Right: stone no. 6 from the west wall, showing two cross-inscribed circles in the lower field (regarded as solar symbols) and half-moon-shaped signs at the top, which are either lunar symbols or representations of ritual axes. Statens Historiska Museum, Stockholm

The sequence of events depicted on the inner walls of the stone tomb from Kivik seems to be a Nordic translation of a funerary ritual represented more accurately in the painted decoration of a sarcophagus from Hagia Triada in Crete (fig. 5). The two are similar not so much in style as in the over-all conception of a pictorial account. The formal parallels are particularly striking. The chariot and the scene around the caldron are the most vividly represented elements in both instances. The interpretation of the scene as a sacrifice is certainly plausible so far as Kivik is concerned. A slender pyramid and ritual axes seem to play a part in both depictions of the ceremony. Such pyramids often stand for gold headpieces (cf. page 92) or ritual columns (cf. figs. 4, 5). They may also be remotely related to the gilded tips of obelisks. The similarities between the scenes from Kivik and Hagia Triada are inconceivable without the assumption of direct contacts and a similar burial ritual, for it is impossible to regard the decorations as meaningless signs (see page 123). The remarkable identity between the Aegean and Nordic imagery is nowhere else manifested so strikingly as in this case, but even so, it discloses the existence of considerable gaps in our knowledge which await further archaeological discovery.

Funerary stele made of a thick stone slab (the anthropomorphic head above the engraved ornamental band is damaged). Height 29³/₄″. From a burial mound at Stockach, Tübingen, Baden-Württemberg, Germany. Württembergisches Landesmuseum, Stuttgart

Slabs with geometric signs from a group around the foot of a burial mound. Sandstone, height 19⁵/₈–21⁵/₈″. From the Mark-Wald, Höchstadt an der Aisch, Bavaria, Germany. Prähistorische Staatssammlung, Munich

Representations of the human figure were taboo for a long time or, it would seem, were allowed only in the case of gods and the dead. However, the images of gods or the dead in the Metal Age do not seem to be direct descendants of the megalithic menhirs, whether the latter were conceived of merely as substitute bodies or characterized by figurative elements. Archaeological evidence for the existence of sculptured poles (such as might have marked an intermediate stage) is hard to come by. What few remains we have of wooden steles from the Hallstatt period erected on burial mounds seem to antedate the early stone steles on which the human figure is at best suggested. On the Stockach stele (facing page, top), only the head has been sculpted to any degree from the flat ashlar. The incised pattern may be formally related to the so-called figure stones which were placed around burial mounds—for example, in the Mark-Wald. What the incised geometric patterns stood for is far from clear, but we can be sure that they were not purely ornamental. Possibly the figure stones signal a tendency to individual expression in a period hostile to representation of the human figure. Not surprisingly, the one large sculpture that has come down to us from the region north of the Alps, the funerary stele from Hirschlanden, dating from the Hallstatt period, clearly discloses Italic influence. It was probably a memorial to the warrior who was buried at the center of the mound. That he was of high rank we can tell from his helmet, dagger, and neck ring (cf. page 98). The portrait exhibits a mixture of classical and barbarian stylistic features. The massive freestanding legs are unique in Prehistoric Europe at this time: they were obviously modeled upon technically crude Etruscan sculpture. At the same time, the upper part of the body is almost a low relief. Clearly, the emblems of rank and the way the figure holds its arms follow some rigid convention. The sculptor was allowed the artistic freedom to follow a classical model in shaping the lower part of the figure, but he was not permitted to depart from tradition in treating symbolic figuration.

Warrior's funerary stele (the feet are missing). Sandstone, height 59″. From a burial mound at Hirschlanden, Leonberg, Baden-Württemberg, Germany. Württembergisches Landesmuseum, Stuttgart

Bowl with human feet. Clay, height excluding handles 3^1/$_8$″. From Lednice, Mikulov, Moravia, Czechoslovakia. Moravian Museum, Brno

Use of the human figure for magical purposes led to the practice of representing individual parts of the human body, such as hands and feet. Thus, the little bowl from Lednice (facing page) was given human legs. This was surely done for some specific reason, idle toying with forms being alien to the Prehistoric potter. Our vessel may possibly fall within the sphere of the caldron rituals. If this conjecture is correct, then we have here a brilliant simplification of the frequently expressed motif of a woman carrying a bowl or kettle on her head. One or another sort of vessel containing a sacred liquid played a part in many ancient cults, its specific role probably varying widely in different regions and periods. That this custom was widespread can be seen from the frequency with which bowls or kettles are represented. The razor handle from Behringstedt, depicting a female figure with stylized ears and earrings and carrying a vessel, has its finest counterparts in Etruria (fig. 3). The motif itself, however, was not confined to Italy and northern Germany. It seems to have originated in southeastern Europe, and there are clay as well as bronze sculptures that make use of it. Thus, the Behringstedt figure would embody forms and functions derived from very different sources. Such superficial assimilation of formal elements is entirely consistent with Prehistoric modes of behavior.

Razor handle in the form of a woman carrying a kettle (one ear is missing). Bronze, height c. 2³/₄″. From Behringstedt, Rendsburg, Schleswig-Holstein, Germany. Nationalmuseet, Copenhagen

Two statuettes of men with movable arms (now missing) and one, probably female, statuette with neck ring. Bronze, height c. 5″. The former from Stockhult, Skåne, Sweden; the latter from Ingelstad, Skåne, Sweden. Statens Historiska Museum, Stockholm

Figurine from Iberia. Bronze, height 5³/₄″. Said to have been discovered with other figures near ▶
Aust-on-Severn, Gloucestershire, England. British Museum, London

The form of a given sculpture was usually determined by its purpose or function.
The bronze statuette from Ingelstad (facing page) unmistakably falls into a category of female deities or ritual figures, found in Denmark and in Etruria, which
must originally have expressed identical meanings in the same, or at least very
similar, forms (cf. fig. 3 and page 140). This is not to say that they bore the same
names and performed the same functions, but that they probably reflect the same
basic mythical conceptions. How such links between the Prehistoric European
religions were forged and how they broke away in the course of time lies beyond
the present scope of our knowledge. All we can be sure of is that Mediterranean
products often reached northern Europe via the British Isles. The limestone drums
from Folkton are early examples of how Iberian art influenced England. The faces
on them are copies of faces on clay pots found in megalithic graves of the Iberian
Peninsula. The faces are merely suggested, as was common in megalithic art, mere
signs indicating the eyes and nose of (presumably) some deity (cf. page 85). Even
after the Carthaginians closed the Straits of Gibraltar to sea traffic in the fifth
century B.C., the ties between Iberia and Britain persisted. As late as the La Tène
epoch, Iberian deities like those found at Aust-on-Severn reached England, where
they were probably also regarded as deities. Moreover, there are striking similarities between the systems of worship in England and Scandinavia, for all the differences between the two regions. The two bronze male statuettes from Stockhult
(facing page) are stylized in a quite original way. The headgear is obviously of a
Mediterranean type, but in essential details the figures are very like the wooden
figures from Roos Carr (page 149). Like the latter, they have movable arms, oversized heads, and elongated, poorly delineated bodies. In both cases, the figures
stand with knees slightly bent, like the dancer from Järrestad (page 126). Such
details suggest that the statuettes reflected similar conceptions.

Decorated drums with stylized faces. Limestone, height c. 4″, 4³/₄″, and 5¹/₂″. From a burial mound
at Folkton, Yorkshire, England. British Museum, London

Two of seven statuettes formerly mounted on a wooden ritual boat. Bronze, height c. 4³/₄″ and 2″. From an unknown site in Denmark. Nationalmuseet, Copenhagen

Horned helmets represent something special in the way of personal accouterment, and their artistic and technical execution is also out of the ordinary. Both of those shown on the facing page exhibit highly stylized faces, not, apparently, intended to inspire fear, in spite of the horns. Obviously, they have to be regarded as signs, as symbolic of some actually imagined face, and as performing a function similar to that of ritual masks. Our suspicion that they must have served as ceremonial regalia is confirmed by the fact that they were buried at hard-to-find spots in the moors and that they occur in pairs—a circumstance that always suggests something special where precious or unusual finds are concerned. The same is true of bronze shields, revealing a curious relationship to the double-shield symbol which is found both in the far North and in the Mediterranean area, e.g., in Sardinia. Generally speaking, the nearest counterparts to the horned helmets of the North are on bronze statuettes found in Sardinia, some of which are holding two shields. To the same group belongs the little statuette of a kneeling man with horned helmet found at an unknown site in Denmark. It was probably part of a wooden ritual boat with several figures in the round representing the enactment of a water rite. The motif of the ship with a helmeted man and another making a backward dive into the water is also known from rock drawings. The helmeted man seems to have played a leading role: his left arm is bent in two sharp angles, and the thumb points upward (cf. page 127). This gesture, in connection with the kneeling position, and the ornamental helmet, must be the key to the figure's significance. The artistic expressiveness derives primarily from the masklike dignity of helmeted man and diver alike. Their features are so schematized as to suggest that those who actually enacted the ritual wore masks.

Ceremonial horned helmets. The headpiece consists of two repoussé halves riveted together; the surmounting horns were cast in ▶ bronze; feathers or tufts of hair were fixed in the longitudinal groove and two small sockets of the cross-shaped mounting over the top; schematized eyes and eyebrows are raised in repoussé on the front of the helmet. Bronze, height (excluding horns) c. 7″. From a bog at Viksø, Zealand, Denmark. Nationalmuseet, Copenhagen

During the Late Hallstatt period, the art of working metal reached its brilliant peak in the Veneto and the eastern Alps. The so-called art of the situla is a direct continuation of Mediterranean prototypes, both in motifs and in technique. At the same time, it has an autonomous character and portrays life in the Hallstatt epoch more vividly and strikingly than any other archaeological find. The animal friezes most often copy earlier models, particularly where they include fabulous creatures. The decorated areas mainly exhibit festive departures from humdrum existence, with ceremonial feasts apparently holding a prominent place. Next in importance are funerary rituals with processions of horsemen, priests, and sacrificial animals. Whatever individuality the figures might singly appear to have is dissipated by the way features are repeated over and over again. Thus, the pictorial narration remains completely impersonal and can freely combine naturalistic motifs, such as a sacrificial animal led by a rope, with mythical motifs, such as the bird of death hovering above it (see facing page).

Flat figurines with dumbbells. Bronze, height 2½″ and 2⅝″. From the *Götzenacker* (a site where burnt offerings were made) at Landeck, Tyrol, Austria. Tiroler Landesmuseum Ferdinandeum, Innsbruck

Female figurine with raised arms. Bronze, height 3⅛″. From the Parzin-Alpe in the Gramais, Tyrol, Austria. Tiroler Landesmuseum Ferdinandeum, Innsbruck

The flat figurines from the Venetian and Illyrian coasts exhibit some of the motifs characteristic of situla art, such as the combat between men with dumbbell-like objects often represented in scenes of celebration. The figure of a woman with arms raised, probably in prayer, seems more archaic (facing page). Eyes, jewelry, and fabric patterns are suggested by the simplest geometric forms. The nature of the sites where they were found points to the votive character of these figures. They come from places high in the mountains which probably served as natural shrines, and even from a site for burnt sacrifices whose name, *Götzenacker* (Field of Idols), still preserves its Prehistoric significance.

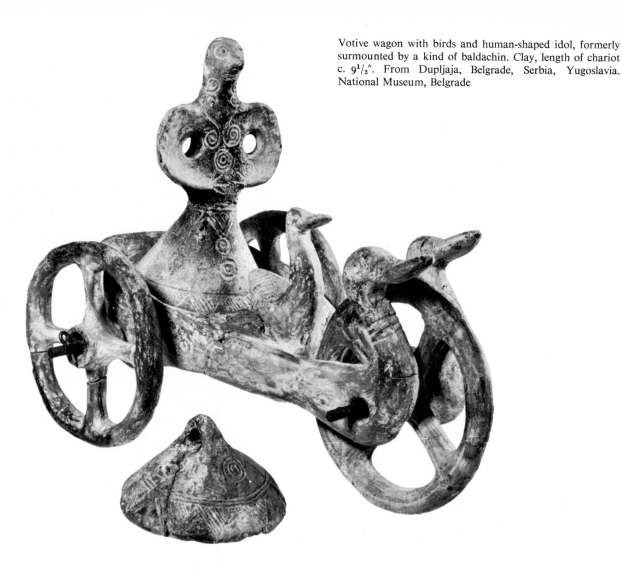

Votive wagon with birds and human-shaped idol, formerly surmounted by a kind of baldachin. Clay, length of chariot c. $9\frac{1}{2}$". From Dupljaja, Belgrade, Serbia, Yugoslavia. National Museum, Belgrade

The purpose of the bronze votive wagons is most often uncertain. The one shown here is probably a combination of symbols rather than the reproduction of a real ritual vehicle. Inside it, beneath the human figure (which lifts out), a solar symbol in the form of a four-spoked wheel is engraved. Accordingly, the figure might stand for Apollo returning from the Hyperboreans, as he did every spring in a chariot drawn by swans. But this is purely conjecture. The peculiar stylization of the figure would classify it rather among the female funerary idols of the northern Balkans (cf. page 66). In fact, all we can say about this find from Dupljaja is that it shows some personified solar deity in a chariot. The underlying belief is a very old, widely held one. It

Wagon with female figure holding up a bowl and stags being led to sacrifice. Bronze, length of chassis 13³/₄″; height of female figure 8⁷/₈″. From an urn field at Strettweg, Styria, Austria. Steiermärkisches Landesmuseum Joanneum, Graz

includes rather than excludes the notion of an afterworld or realm of the dead. Elsewhere, the same belief was associated with a boat rather than a wagon (cf. page 95), or with the horse as a mythical draft animal (page 121). Thus, the Dupljaja wagon neither anticipates a later Greek myth nor does it indicate the birthplace of the myth. Rather, it is one specific Balkan embodiment of a religious idea that enjoyed currency throughout the ancient world. Similar observations apply to the ritual wagon from Strettweg (page 147). Technically and formally, it is related to vehicles in which bowls or basins supported by crossed poles are mounted on the chassis. Such vehicles have no floor boards or sculptured accessories. Similar vehicles are found in richly furnished warriors' graves from the Bronze Age to the Hallstatt epoch over an area extending southwest from Hungary into Italy and north to Scandinavia. The bowls or basins were obviously filled with some consecrated liquid, an *aqua vitae* for use by the dead man in the afterworld. The oversized central figure holding the bowl in the wagon from Strettweg is usually interpreted as a fertility goddess, possibly corresponding to the Nordic female figures carrying vessels (page 137). It is impossible to say anything more specific on this score; in fact we do not even know whether the figure represents the fertility goddess herself or merely a priestess of her cult. The size of the figure provides us with no clue. Its unusually slender shape does not serve as a stylistic device in this instance: it seems purely ornamental, though it is certain that, in the scene represented, it plays a leading part. Like the figure from Dupljaja, it is standing on an engraved solar disk, and so serves as a link between the symbols of sun and bowl. This would seem to be the leitmotiv here: the association of fertility and funerary rites invariably involved the sacrifice of a stag.

Ritual boat with men wielding axes. Rock drawing. Tanum, Bohuslän, Sweden

Stylized boat in the form of a snake with four male figures having movable arms and small shields. Wood with inlaid quartz eyes, length of boat c. 20″. From Roos Carr, Holderness, Yorkshire, England. Museum, Hull

Boats also served as ritual vehicles, though this motif was very variously treated in different times and places and was by no means employed only by peoples living close to the sea. Just what function they served is often impossible to ascertain (cf. page 140). In Egyptian painting, we recognize the gods by their attributes, which are uniform and consistent, whereas in the realm of Prehistory, even the presumed attributes are a matter for debate. For instance, the men on the boat from Tanum (facing page) are holding large axes, but these may not be attributes of ax-gods—they could be ritual axes being wielded by masked men. The schematic arrangement of the figures in the snake-shaped boat from Roos Carr brings to mind certain Egyptian representations (cf. also page 139). The armed figures may well be deities, but it is just as possible that they symbolize dead men. In any case, other finds at the same site suggest that this boat has some connection with graves and

Oval bowl with stylized carvings and ornamental mountings, which served as a votive boat. The remains of the band around the rim bear concentric circle motifs which may represent shields. Oak and gold, length 7¹/₄″. From a formerly boggy site at Caergwrle, Hope, Flintshire, Wales. National Museum of Wales, Cardiff

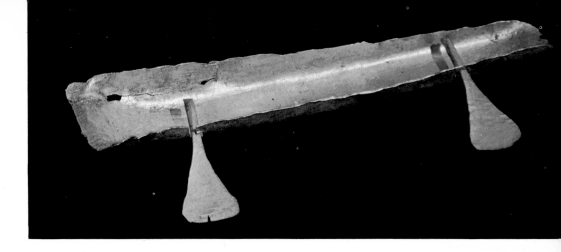

Votive boat with two oars. Thin sheet gold, length c. 2″. From a grave
on the Dürrnberg, Hallein, Salzburg, Austria. Museum, Hallein

Votive boats. Pressed gold leaf, length 3⁷/₈″. About one hundred of these tiny boats were
found in a clay vessel at Nors, Nordthy, Denmark. Nationalmuseet, Copenhagen

the afterworld. Near Roos Carr, similar boats manned by wooden crews were actually launched. Thus, they may have symbolized a voyage of the dead. Wherever the gods of myth were supposed to have come from the sea or other water, it was believed the dead must journey back to that place to rejoin them. Notions of an underground river, of the Isles of the Blessed, and of a ferryman transporting the dead are not confined to Greek mythology. Such a crossing of water is represented in the La Tène period in the boatman from Magdalensberg (page 232). Interment in coffin-boats and in boat-shaped stone alignments culminated in Viking Scandinavia in the ship-tombs of kings and chieftains. The basic idea was soon disengaged from the personal image and embodied in the symbolic boat. This inevitably led to the use of more valuable materials and to more careful treatment. What the boats from Tanum and Roos Carr (pages 148, 149) stood for must have been obvious to their contemporaries. Although drawing and sculpture are realistic, in keeping with the current modes of representation, they were not intended as works of art. However, where the scenes represented provide no clues, we must interpret them as symbolic or ornamental. Ritual and artistic requirements are best reconciled in purely craft works, i.e., those which lack figural representation. Precious raw materials possess intrinsic value; thus, the tiny gold boat from Hallein (page 151) must have been regarded as a more powerful symbol than boats made of ordinary materials. The same applies to the miniature gold-leaf boats from Nors (page 151). Hundreds of such boats offered to the gods above and below the waters were intended to secure a happy voyage for the dead on their way from this world to the next. The fact that they may date from Roman Imperial times is irrelevant in this connection. One of the oldest and most elaborate votive boats seems to be the bowl from Caergwrle (page 150).

Crested helmet with ornamental bosses. Bronze, height c. 12″. From the Tanaro at Asti, Piedmont, Italy. Museo Civico, Turin

Cuirass. Repoussé sheet bronze, height c. 19½″. From the Saône at Saint-Germain-du-Plain (Saône-et-Loire), France. Musée des Antiquités Nationales, Saint-Germain-en-Laye

The various regions of Prehistoric Europe had contacts with the ancient Mediterranean world at different times and assimilated its influence in a variety of ways, depending on the closeness of the contacts as well as on economic factors. In this respect, objects that belonged to the ruling classes are the most instructive. Only the rich and powerful could afford helmets and chest armor. Besides outfitting themselves with such badges of rank, the upper classes also adopted ways and modes of social organization which eventually gave rise to an early form of feudalism. During the Age of Metals, Central Europe must

have gone through the same phases as the Aegean world in its age of heroes, depicted later in Greek literature. But Europe as a whole had not yet emerged from Prehistory: it remained essentially barbaric and culturally dependent upon the older advanced civilizations and their Mediterranean successors. This is why Prehistoric sites that yielded objects imported from Magna Graecia stand out sharply from the rest and are easily recognizable as having been centers of local government. Around 500 B.C., a princess was buried at a fortified settlement on Mont Lassois, near Vix, and into her grave went a splendid carriage, personal adornments of bronze and gold, and Greek tableware. A bronze crater found in the burial chamber probably came from a Greek workshop; it was made specially for the princess or her family. Its immoderate size is characteristic of barbaric taste or, more accurately, of the Greek craftsmen's idea of it. Huge vessels for mixing wine are recorded in historical tradition: the Spartans, for instance, presented Croesus, king of Lydia, with such a vessel. An outstanding import from the classical world such as the Vix crater helps us to grasp how backward the rest of Europe still was—and not only in respect of art and the crafts.

Large crater with volute handles terminating in snake-footed gorgons. A relief frieze around the neck of the vessel (detail below) shows hoplites and horse-drawn war chariots. Bronze, height 64⁵/₈″; weight c. 460 lbs. Greek import; from the grave of a princess at Vix, near Châtillon-sur-Seine (Côte-d'Or), France. Musée Archéologique, Châtillon-sur-Seine

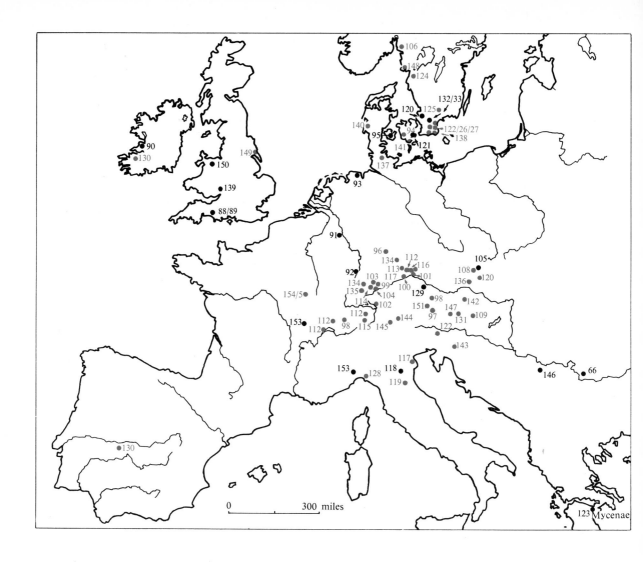

Bronze Age and Early Iron Age sites

Red: Hallstatt (stages C and D), Late Bronze Age (periods V and VI). To Hallstatt p. 97 should be added pp. 107, 110, 111 (omitted from the map for lack of space).

There are two explanations for the fact that so many finds come from Central Europe, the Alps, and the Danube Valley: firstly, these regions were strongly influenced from the southeast (though the widely scattered sites do not reflect this fact); and secondly, the Hallstatt period was more receptive to new pictorial motifs than older periods. Contacts with the North and with Central Italy, especially in Late Hallstatt times, are not properly reflected here. At this time, there was lively trade with Greek colonies all along the northern Mediterranean coast, which ought, theoretically, to be indicated on the map in order to provide a complete picture. In fact, this map complements the concentration of Hallstatt finds indicated on the chart on the facing page; it does not attempt to show the actual divisions into zones and groups of Prehistoric times.

Chronological chart of the Bronze Age and Early Iron Age

The numbers refer to pages. Where the dating is uncertain, a question mark has been added to the page reference. EBA = Early Bronze Age; MBA = Middle Bronze Age; LBA = Late Bronze Age.

Because each area developed at a different pace, several, sometimes very different, chronological systems have been devised. There are, however, some points of agreement where successive stages of development are concerned. For Central Europe and its peripheral zones, the currently accepted division goes back to P. Reinecke. He named the entire period following the Bronze Age the "Hallstatt epoch," after a grave site near Hallstatt in the Salzkammergut. Later, the first two stages of the Hallstatt (A and B) were considered to be a separate period and were called the "Urn Field period," after the custom of cremation prevailing at the time. For the north of Europe—Scandinavia and northern Germany—one can use the system of O. Montelius, which breaks the period down into six parts. Like Reinecke's system, it was later revised and is now sometimes made to include subdivisions which primarily concern the smaller geographical areas. As for the British Isles, no single system of classification seems possible. Where southern England is concerned, we have followed the division proposed by C. F. C. Hawkes and others. Dating is based partly on comparisons between groups, but to a greater extent on imports from the Mediterranean area. These include the gold cup from Fritzdorf (p. 91), which is an imitation of a Mycenaean vessel. The Late Hallstatt period can be quite precisely dated on the basis of Greek imports: the royal grave at Vix, for instance, can confidently be dated c. 500 B.C. Iron made its appearance as early as the Urn Field period (stage A) but did not become an important economic factor until the Hallstatt. The large number of Hallstatt finds is no accident—this period was marked by a flowering of the crafts and an increase in the number of representational motifs, often exhibiting Mediterranean influences.

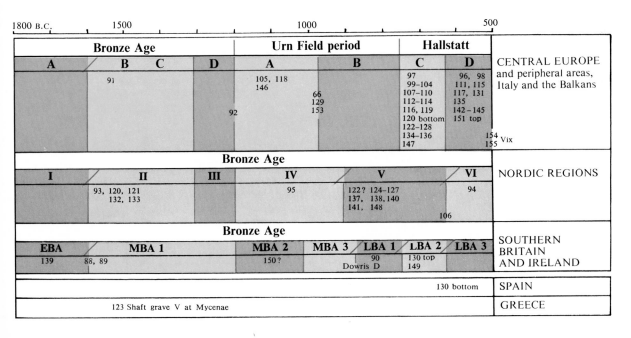

1800 B.C.　　1500　　　　　1000　　　　　500

Bronze Age				Urn Field period		Hallstatt		CENTRAL EUROPE and peripheral areas, Italy and the Balkans
A	B	C	D	A	B	C	D	
	91		92	105, 118 146	66 129 153	97 99–104 107–110 112–114 116, 119 120 bottom 122–128 134–136 147	96, 98 111, 115 117, 131 135 142–145 151 top	154 155 Vix

Bronze Age						NORDIC REGIONS
I	II	III	IV	V	VI	
	93, 120, 121 132, 133		95	122? 124–127 137, 138, 140 141, 148　　106	94	

Bronze Age							SOUTHERN BRITAIN AND IRELAND
EBA	MBA 1	MBA 2	MBA 3	LBA 1	LBA 2	LBA 3	
139	88, 89	150?		90 Dowris D	130 top 149		

	SPAIN
130 bottom	

	GREECE
123 Shaft grave V at Mycenae	

Entrance to the Chamber of the Pillared Niches, South
Temple of Mnaidra, Malta. The huge stone slabs are fitted
together with great care, and the pitting of the surface is
a form of ornamentation. Mnaidra is a temple site on the
south coast of the island, today largely in ruins. It comprises three major structures, each containing several
chambers, some of them articulated by pillars and niches.
They were erected at different times during Malta's
Prehistory, corresponding roughly to Europe's Early
Bronze Age. Systematic excavation began in 1954

Bull's Head (two views). Bronze. From Costig, Majorca.
Museo Arqueológico Nacional, Madrid

THE WESTERN MEDITERRANEAN

The western Mediterranean fell under the influence of the advanced Eastern cultures at an early stage of its
development. From the Neolithic period on, a steady stream of material goods, ideas, pictorial motifs, and
techniques flowed from east to west. Long before the Phoenicians and the Greeks, the western coastal regions
had been plundered and enriched by sailors of other races. How the local arts and crafts were affected can
here be briefly suggested by a few illustrations. Which Eastern influence predominated at a given moment
varied according to which power controlled the land and sea trade routes at the time. The Roman victory over
Carthage in 202 B.C., followed by the conquest of Spain a few years later, marked the elimination of the Greeks
and the Carthaginians (successors to the Phoenicians) from the political history of the western Mediterranean.

Down to this time, however, typically Eastern religious ideas and ways of life had prevailed there. Worship of the bull, for example, had long since been introduced and had taken on characteristic forms in Prehistoric times among the peoples of the Iberian Peninsula, where vestiges of it survive to this day in the bullfight. On the other hand, the western islands, though accessible by sea, were often cut off from other cultures, particularly those that lay to one side of the customary trade routes and remained apart from the mainland struggles for political power. Thus it came about that elements common to the Mediterranean region took on highly peculiar forms on the islands. The megalithic monuments of the Bronze Age in Malta can serve as a case in point. Such structural features as the temple entrance illustrated here were borrowed from Crete and Mycenae, but the linking of sanctuary and tomb, the cyclopean structures divided into chambers, and the laborious pitted ornamentation of the gateway such as we find at Mnaidra are not encountered anywhere but in Malta.

Statuette of a warrior with bow and arrow, wearing a short tunic, ▶
leather greaves, and a helmet (originally with horns, now missing).
Bronze. From an unknown site in Sardinia. Museo Archeologico,
Cagliari

Sardinia is rich in archaeological monuments of all kinds. Among them, the bronzes take first place for the abundance of their motifs and details. The reason no figure is exactly like another is probably that they were cast by the lost-wax technique. They were set up as votive offerings at special sites. Traces of lead on the feet show that the bronzes were fastened to supports of some kind. Most of them date from the first half of the

first millennium B.C. The development of Phoenician trade in this period accounts for the diffusion of various types of objects, such as Late Bronze Age armor. In Sardinia, however, leather greaves were worn rather than bronze ones. The statuettes supply us with many such details of costume, arms, and implements. But the special charm of the island's art derives from the fact that each small sculpture is unique—in marked contrast to the mass-produced sculpture of the Iberian Peninsula and elsewhere (cf. pages 164–65). What Sardinian art, nonetheless, has in common with Iberian is the fact that, nearly always, it is the life of the group that is portrayed, not that of individuals.

◀ Statuettes, identified by the hat (or round cap), cloak, and raised right arm as chieftains or clan elders, whose dignity and rank are usually stressed by a long staff held in the left hand. Bronze, height 8″ (left) and 6³/₄″. From an unknown site in Sardinia. National-museet, Copenhagen

"Grotesque" mask, intended to frighten off evil spirits. Terra cotta, life-size. From Tharros (present-day Capo San Marco). British Museum, London

The Phoenicians were in contact with so many other peoples that their art exhibits a mixture of foreign styles and techniques. One specifically Phoenician feature, however, is the palmette design around the clasp of the gold belt from Aliseda. It was found together with other Phoenician treasure near Gades (present-day Cádiz), a trading outpost of Tartessos, an Iberian kingdom which had close contacts with the Phoenicians from the eighth century B.C. on, and which was at times politically subject to them. After the rise of the Punic Empire, Greek, Etruscan, and Iberian models were introduced, though Phoenician works continued to be imitated. Only a few implements exhibit a specifically Western style; most of these were destined for religious or magical purposes and are often of slight artistic quality. The grotesque terra-cotta masks belong in this category. They have been found in Carthage itself, and in Ibiza and Sardinia. The last-mentioned was occupied militarily by the Carthaginians following the battle of Alalia in 535 B.C. The masks may reflect some African influence: they often show tattooing.

Phoenician belt (detail) with granulation, figures and ornamentation in repoussé. Gold, over-all length of belt 27″; width of clasp 2³/₄″. From Aliseda, Cáceres, Spain. Museo Arqueológico Nacional, Madrid

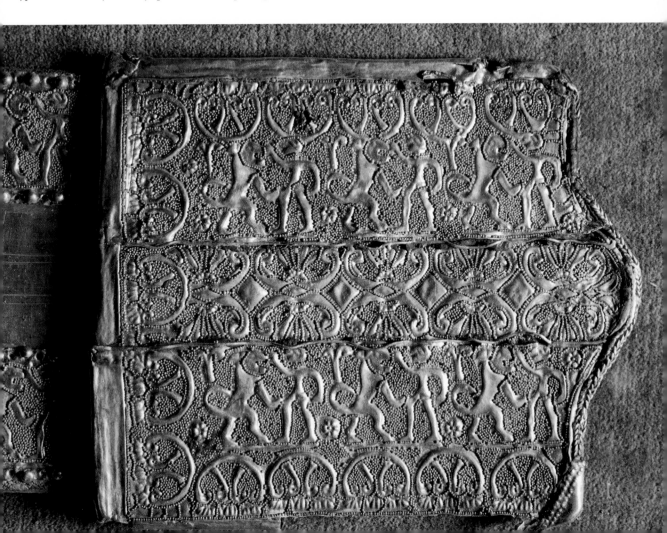

Iberian statuettes. Man in tunic with pomegranates (?) (left), warrior in tunic and helmet (middle), and woman wearing a mantilla (right). Bronze, height $3^7/_8''$, $10^1/_4''$, and $3^7/_8''$ respectively. From the sanctuary of El Collado de los Jardines, Despeñaperros, Jaén, Spain. Museo Arqueológico Nacional, Madrid

The fate of the Iberian Peninsula was essentially determined by settlers who came by sea. In the first millennium B.C., however, several waves of Celtic tribes moved in by land from the east. Under their influence, new forms of culture took root and developed, though the Mediterranean influences never disappeared. Even at this time, the Iberians exhibited a distinctive religiosity, or at least a marked attachment to ritual. This is reflected in the large number of temples they built and by the quantities of sacrificial and votive offerings. The variety and quality of the latter probably reflect the relative importance of the different individual sanctuaries and the deities to whom they were dedicated. Thus, in Andalusia, the bronze statuettes found at temple sites seem to have been mass-produced. A few were chased, and a very few exhibit classical features. In most cases, the figures are of human beings, with a preponderance of warriors both mounted and on foot. The majority appear to have been produced between the fourth century B.C. and the Roman conquest. The three statuettes from El Collado de los Jardines come from a temple built on artificial terraces which was destroyed during Hannibal's campaign.

The temple at El Cigarralejo stood on a hill. Its stone sculptures are chiefly of horses, with a few donkeys. Carved from rectangular or cylindrical stone blocks, the animals are perfectly executed in naturalistic style. The horse shown on page 167 is the work of the so-called *Maestro del Cigarralejo,* who was apparently attached to the temple. All the evidence would indicate that the temple was dedi-

Head of a Woman. Stone, height 16¼″. From the temple at Cerro de los Santos, Albacete, Spain. Museo Arqueológico Nacional, Madrid

cated to a horse-goddess, perhaps the Celtic Epona. The sculptures probably do not represent the goddess herself in the guise of a horse, worship of a mother-goddess being obviously more important at this time. The votive bronzes associated with the latter most often represent the donors themselves (see page 165). Still more frequent are sculptures in stone. The sanctuary at Cerro de los Santos alone yielded more than three hundred sculptures, either fully executed figures (page 168) or abbreviated to only the heads and busts of the donors. They achieve especially high artistic quality when they show traces of Greek influence; for instance, certain alabaster heads capped with the high Iberian bonnet clearly exhibit features of Archaic Greek art. Though idealized and rigorously stylized, every donor's portrait was individually conceived (see pages 168, 171). In view of the populous Greek colonies along the Spanish coast, the presence of Greek stylistic features is hardly surprising. At Cerro de los Santos, for instance, two Ionic capitals adorned the portico of a large treasury, and therefore date the building to the fifth century B.C.

Votive Horse. Sandstone, length c. 8″. From the temple at El Cigarralejo, Murcia, Spain. Collection E. Cuadrado, Madrid

Statue of a Woman. Stone, height 37⅜". From the sanctuary at Cerro de los Santos, Albacete, Spain. Museo Arqueológico Nacional, Madrid

Iberian sculpture seems to have been influenced little, if at all, by Carthaginian work, perhaps because of prior exposure to Greek art. Furthermore, the characteristic motifs are different. Carthaginian sculptures often represent a deity or the figure of someone who has died. The clay mask of a woman from Ibiza (facing page) belongs in the same category of representation as the anthropomorphic Carthaginian sarcophagi of clay or stone, the purpose of which was to ensure the dead man's existence in the afterworld through preservation of his features. This concern for the welfare of the dead, an eastern Mediterranean attitude, had a counterpart in the votive offerings of the Iberians, although the archaeological evidence is still far from clear on this point. The alabaster statuette of a Phoenician fertility goddess (page 170) dating from the seventh or sixth century B.C. was discovered near Galera in a grave which dates from a much later time, perhaps from the fourth century B.C. This shows that images of the type did not lose all significance and were probably used for magical purposes. But for all their indebtedness to Greek prototypes, the Iberian sculptors developed a certain originality, probably quite consciously. The large sculptures retain archaic features: they are like steles. This may, in part, be accounted for by the sacred character of the themes treated, which would have demanded adherence to traditional forms. The cloaked and hooded lady from the sanctuary at Cerro de los Santos probably represents a pilgrim. The way in which she is holding some kind of vessel is treated in an identical manner in all such sculptures from this site, but costume and jewelry are varied in accordance with the living model. In the work shown here, the sensitive face stands out in vivid contrast to the schematized treatment of the costume. One of the female statues is no less richly accoutered than the so-called *Lady of Elche* (page 171), a bust which was probably also destined to be set up in a temple. Its artistic appeal lies in the contrast between the limpid classical treatment of the face and the barbaric wealth of ornamental detail, between idealization and naturalism.

Plaque with female face in relief. Clay. From the Punic necropolis of ▶ Puig d'es Molins, Ibiza. Museo Arqueológico, Barcelona

The Lady of Elche, bust of an elaborately attired woman. Painted limestone, height 10¹/₄″. From La Alcudia de Elche, Alicante, Spain. The Prado, Madrid

◀ Statuette of a Phoenician fertility goddess. Alabaster, height 7″. From Tutugi (present-day Galera), Granada, Spain. Museo Arqueológico Nacional, Madrid

The classical world also influenced the ceramic products of more backward regions. Light-colored porous pottery was produced with the aid of a primitive potter's wheel in many local workshops. Simple geometric patterns were favored, enlivened by the use of oval, spiral, and bladderlike ornamentation. It is hardly possible to distinguish between design and background, any more than it is in the metalwork of the eastern Celts (cf. page 199). Apart from actual scenes, representation of humans and animals falls within the category of ornament. In contrast to classical prototypes, human bodies are mostly given in frontal view, the limbs in profile. The legs of the horseman on the *Warriors' Vase* from Archena are drawn as though they were both on the same side of the horse (cf. fig. 6).

Warriors' Vase, painted funerary urn. Height 15³/₄″. From a grave site at Archena, Murcia, Spain. Museo Arqueológico Nacional, Madrid

Female Figure, detail of an amphora. Painted clay. ▶ From La Alcudia de Elche, Alicante, Spain. Collection R. Folques, Elche

◀ Pitcher from a grave site containing cremated remains. Painted clay, height 15¹/₈″. From Cebecico des Tesoro, grave 213, Verdolay, Murcia, Spain. Museo Arqueológico Nacional, Madrid

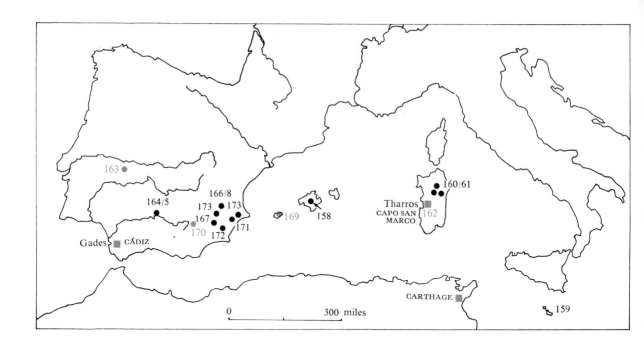

Western Mediterranean sites

Red: Phoenician and Carthaginian (Punic) finds.

The small number of find sites indicated on the map can give no real idea of cultural connections and developments in the area. The map (which is only intended to reflect the illustrations in this book) omits the Greek colonies along the Iberian coast, which exerted a powerful influence on Celtic stone sculpture in this region (cf. pp. 166, 168, 171). Nor can the map show adequately the routes of Phoenician trade and of Carthaginian political expansion. Finds from Ibiza (p. 169) and from Tharros in Sardinia (p. 162) are the only evidence illustrated in this book for the expansionism of the Carthaginians in this part of the world from the seventh century B.C. on. Most other sites indicated refer to temples and votive offerings, and cover a time span stretching from the Bronze Age to the Middle La Tène. Celtic influences appear only in southeastern Spain.

Chronological chart of the western Mediterranean region

The numbers refer to pages. Where the dating is uncertain, a question mark has been added to the page reference. The more thickly shaded areas indicate the absolute age of the finds in question.

The chart shows only a few of the cultural phenomena of this region. Some of the oldest still await more thorough study, above all, those on Malta. The kind of imagery involved shows that most of the works date from periods for which historical records exist. The Nuraghic culture of Sardinia, however, is still entirely Prehistoric. The name comes from a type of towerlike stone structure (*nuraghe*), which was normally used as a dwelling and, in times of trouble, was enlarged and fortified. The increase in sea trade clearly had some influence on this culture; such trade had been started by the Phoenicians who, as early as the twelfth century B.C., had established trading posts on the Spanish coast. They founded Gades, present-day Cádiz. In the eighth century B.C., Greek colonies made their appearance. The Celts came from the east in several waves and founded peculiarly Iberian Celtic settlements, for instance, at Tartessos, a kingdom in the southwest of the peninsula. The beginnings of this kingdom are buried in the mists of legend, but it is known to have survived down to the fourth century B.C. Meanwhile, the Carthaginians kept extending their sphere of influence. The western Phoenicians founded Carthage in 814 B.C.; as early as 654/653, they were in possession of Ibiza; and in 535, parts of Sardinia were theirs also. A succession of wars in which Carthaginians, Greeks, Etruscans, and Romans were involved led to the First Punic War (264–261 B.C.), which brought an end to the Greek colonies. The Second Punic War ended with the destruction of Carthage in 202 B.C., after Scipio's decisive victory over Hannibal at Zama. From then on, Rome held sway over the western Mediterranean.

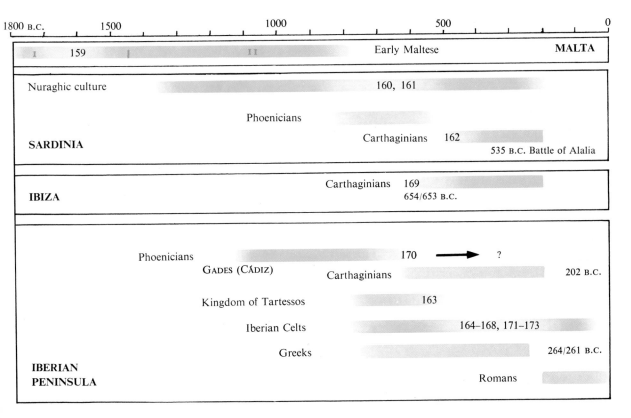

Pieces of harness dating from the Early Hallstatt period. Bronze. Top and bottom: cheekpieces from Beilngries, Bavaria, Germany, length $5^1/_4''$. Right: snaffle from Lengenfeld, Parsberg, Bavaria, Germany, length $5^3/_8''$. Center: cross-shaped terrets from München-Pullach, Bavaria, Germany, length c. 1″. Prähistorische Staatssammlung, Munich

Down to the close of the Middle Ages, Europe was repeatedly invaded by mounted nomadic peoples from the East. Not all of these peoples, however, were simply predators who made off with all they could carry, never to return. The earliest such invaders settled down and merged with the indigenous populations, and because they kept in contact with one another, contributed to the circulation of goods and ideas in areas that had remained at Prehistoric stages of development. At the same time, they were themselves brought into touch with the ancient societies of the Aegean and the Black Sea. The earliest archaeological finds in southeastern Europe that can be connected with historical events date from the second half of the eighth century B.C. North of the Black Sea, the Cimmerians were driven out by the Scythians. One group of the former moved across the Caucasus into Asia Minor, while other groups pushed westward into Thrace, probably driving already settled

Statuette of man on horseback. Clay, length $3^1/_8''$.
From a burial mound at Speikern, Lauf an der
Pegnitz, Bavaria, Germany. Collection of the
Naturhistorische Gesellschaft, Nuremberg

tribes along with them. Eventually, this movement of peoples reached East and South Germany and North and Central Italy. Everywhere this occurred, new political configurations sprang up, ruled, or at least influenced, by the warlike spirit of the nomads from the East. Though ultimately they merged with the already settled peoples of the lands they invaded, the nomad strain occasionally preserved its identity as a distinct social class. This development can be inferred from numerous changes in the character of archaeological finds. The routes followed by the nomads are most readily traceable on the basis of specific types of bronze harness, the ultimate origin of which was in the region north of the Black Sea. Among other identifying characteristics are the comparatively small snaffles, the slightly curved cheekpieces, and the cross-shaped terrets. The leading position enjoyed by an upper class of horsemen or knights is reflected in the art of these peoples. One of the earliest Hallstatt sculptures, signaling the emergence of an entirely new world of images, is a tiny horse (the size of a finger) with rider. It would be a mistake, however, to regard this as a purely "barbarian" art, for it clearly exhibits Greek influences (noticeable particularly in drawings and small sculptures), probably picked up by the nomads in the course of their wanderings. In Greece itself at this time, sculptures of horses came to the fore, above all as votive offerings. The little horse from Speikern, like its Central European counterparts (cf. page 114), is unmistakably a crude copy of Geometric clay horses (cf. fig. 8).

Scepter in the form of a club with horse's head. Bronze,
length 4³/₄". From the Sárvíz Canal at Tolna, Hungary.
Hungarian National Museum, Budapest

Horse-shaped clubs symbolized the power and authority of the horsemen. The numbers of such clubs found in Hungary and Bohemia show not merely that the mounted nomads of the Hallstatt epoch had got this far west, but also that they were settling down to a sufficient extent among the peoples they conquered to produce metalwork in some quantity. The club-scepter on the facing page comes from the grave of a nomadic chieftain, but all the other grave furnishings were of the kind used by the indigenous populations. Conversely, the indigenous groups were at this time being influenced by Eastern ideas and imagery. The ceremonial ax from Hallstatt, for instance, which is basically just another version of the horse-headed scepter, does not achieve the elegant stylization of the latter. The scepter linked use or function with ornament and symbolic meaning organically: the mounted figure on the Hallstatt ax is no more than a superfluous afterthought on the sculptor's part. As so often with works from the Hallstatt period, we realize that we are dealing with rather inexperienced artists and craftsmen (cf. page 111). Quite apart from the formal failure, the Hallstatt ax was clearly produced under very different artistic conditions from the scepter. But the motif of the man on horseback on the ax shows that the imagery of the newcomers had become acceptable to the natives.

Ceremonial ax with figure of a horse and rider. Bronze, length 4″. From Hallstatt, grave 641, Upper Austria. Naturhistorisches Museum, Vienna

Horses and Riders. Drawing on a clay vessel done by the roulette technique, height of figures $1^5/_8$". From Beilngries, Bavaria, Germany. Prähistorische Staatssammlung, Munich

▼

Horses and Riders. Rock drawings, length
4³/₄–8⁵/₈″. Järrestad, Skåne, Sweden

The Hallstatt or Late Bronze Age motif of the horseman spread to the farthest corners of Europe with astonishing speed. Needless to say, treatment varies greatly from place to place, depending on available materials and local artistic traditions. Nevertheless, a few basic features are common to all. On the clay vessel from Beilngries (facing page), use of the roulette gives a linear, geometric treatment to the motif (cf. page 116). The men seem to be standing on the horses' backs, the reins around their own heads. Here, the oddly linear treatment renders the three essential elements of the motif—horse, reins, and man—but the combination has been effected rather arbitrarily. Although the elements are linked physically, they are not integrated artistically (cf. pages 115, 116 and figs. 6, 7). The work could not possibly have been intended as the depiction of an actual event. The same is true of the rock drawings at Järrestad, although the treatment of the reins is a more nearly accurate depiction. As realistic representation, however, the rock drawings are even wider of the mark. Men on horseback are represented more realistically later in the Hallstatt epoch, when the artists, as they had in the art of the situla, had absorbed the lessons of their ancient Greek models.

Detail of the upper frieze on the bronze situla from Vače, Carniola, Yugoslavia (cf. page 143). National Museum, Ljubljana

A few elaborately worked pieces in gold give an exaggerated idea of Scythian influence in Central Europe. Actually, Scythian culture flowered in southern Russia, but left no permanent mark on the West. The Scythian objects found in Central Bulgaria, Transylvania, and Central Hungary are not evidence of Scythian colonization, but of lively trade between these lands and the Scythians. Only in Bulgaria do we find a few graves strictly comparable to the impressive burial mounds—the kurgans—of Scythian princes at sites north of the Black Sea. Although, from the sixth century B.C. on, the Scythians made predatory incursions westward, perhaps even farther west than Central Germany, specifically Scythian influence on native Western styles really comes down to very little; and that little is confined to the Lower Danube. Among such influences can be counted ornamental harness plaques in lead found in Early La Tène graves in Slovenia which derive from Scythian silver disks used for a similar purpose. The plaque illustrated consists of four horses' heads in a swastika formation. The fact that this particular animal was chosen from the large number of Scythian motifs seems significant, for the horse, so common in European art, plays only a subordinate part in that of the Scythians. The latter's favorite themes are not domestic animals but big game, such as lions, which are not native to the Black Sea region.

Plaque consisting of four horses' heads. Lead. From grave 31 of burial mound 5, near Magdalenska Gora, Smarje, Slovenia, Yugoslavia. Peabody Museum, Cambridge, Mass.

Stag. Stamped gold, length 9″. From Zöldhalompuszta, Pest, Hungary. Hungarian National Museum, Budapest

A distinctive feature of Scythian animal sculpture is the use of sharp-edged curves to delimit individual planes. This produces an effect of tautness which is often further emphasized by inversion, i.e., by turning the animal's head to the back. At the same time, the artists exaggerate the features that suggest strength, such as fangs, jaws, or, as in the stag shown here, antlers. These peculiarities may go back to older chip-carved figures in wood and bone, where only a limited surface was available. Eventually the technique was applied to gold and bronze with the help of pressing molds. This would suggest that the Scythian style derives from the naturalism of the Paleolithic hunters which survived down into the Age of Metals among Asiatic hunters. So long an evolutionary development, for all the gaps in the archaeological record, may explain why the source and origin of Scythian and related animal styles are still matters for debate. The question is further complicated by the fact that the Scythian style was carried to extremes under foreign influence and, unlike Paleolithic art, culminated in purely decorative treatment of animal figures.

Scabbard mounting for a short sword (*akinakes*). Gold, length 7¹/₂″. From the Scythian hoard at Vettersfelde, Guben, Cottbus, Brandenburg, Germany. Museum für Vor- und Frühgeschichte, Berlin

Fish-shaped mounting. Gold, length 16¹/₈″. From the Scythian hoard at Vettersfelde, Guben, Cottbus, Brandenburg, Germany. Museum für Vor- und Frühgeschichte, Berlin

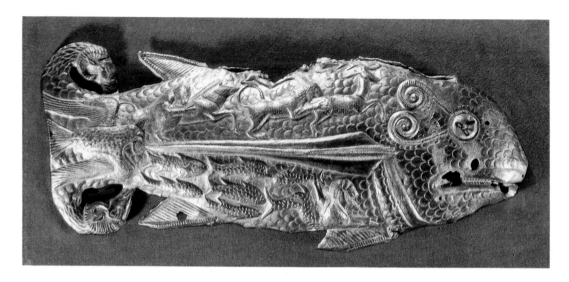

Ornamental plaque. Sheet gold, height 6³/₄″. From the Scythian hoard at Vettersfelde, Guben, Cottbus, Brandenburg, Germany. Museum für Vor- und Frühgeschichte, Berlin

The objects found in the Vettersfelde hoard probably belonged to a Scythian chieftain, and are believed to be the work of Greek craftsmen. Though dazzling enough, the hoard conveys but an imperfect idea of the tremendous wealth of the Pontic princes. Like other nomads, the Scythians employed foreign craftsmen; however, the basic themes and styles of ornamentation are their own, although some motifs and technical innovations came from Greece and Asia Minor. For instance, the grouping of the animals on the quatrefoil mounting shown here derives from Greek models. The lions depicted on the gold scabbard (facing page) are of Near Eastern origin (the rosette was a widely used eastern Mediterranean ornament). Similarly, the lion killing a deer on the fish-shaped mounting has its prototypes in the Mediterranean region. The arrangement of the animals on all three mountings is purely decorative. The frequent use of animal figures for ornamental purposes eventually gave rise to such hybrids as this fish, whose tail fins terminate in rams' heads.

Stag. Mounting in electrum, length c. 8¹/₂". From Tápiószentmárton, Pest, Hungary. Hungarian National Museum, Budapest

The Scythians' predilection for certain animal figures, such as the stag, may have been motivated by consider-
ations of magic. Its ornamental exaggeration would then also have heightened the magical power of the
image and reinforced an art subordinated to magic. This interpretation, however, remains as uncertain as the
origin of most Scythian motifs. The stags and ibexes portrayed on metal mountings, with legs drawn up under
the body and antlers or horns flat against the back, are faithful copies of the earliest Scythian animal figures
on wooden and bone staffs. But no one is sure about the origins of this style of animal sculpture, some of
which goes back to the earliest phases of Scythian history: the ultimate models of the animals with legs drawn
up under their bodies could have originated in Asia Minor just as plausibly as in Central Asia. The characteristic position may be that of animals awaiting sacrifice, legs and antlers bound. And even if this interpretation were correct so far as the origin of the treatment is concerned, it need not apply to the Scythian imitations. That the figures are tightly fitted into a small space with almost unbroken outlines is more readily
accounted for by their ornamental function and by the fact that they appear on metal mountings. The antlers
of the stag from Tápiószentmárton provide an extreme example of ornamental treatment. The foreshortening
of the branch on the right produces an almost perspective effect of the kind that is also produced when the
animal's head is turned backward (cf. page 183).

Many other peoples or tribes followed in the footsteps of the Scythians. If the phalera from the shores of
the Black Sea (facing page) really dates from the second century B.C., it is more or less contemporary with the
Sarmatians' main westward thrust. The phalera is an ornamental disk worn on horses' heads or chests; the
one illustrated may have belonged to a nomadic chieftain, but it exhibits no specifically Sarmatian features.
In the Black Sea region, Greek motifs and techniques survived well into Roman Imperial times, and local
craftsmen also drew upon the store of motifs that nomadic horsemen had in part brought from Central Asia,
in part borrowed from the advanced civilizations in Asia Minor. Princely patrons could choose their motifs
from an abundant collection of original and mixed forms, and even in Greek workshops these were combined
in new ways to meet barbarian demands. The way images were brought together in a single pattern of ornament, whatever their former function or place of origin, no doubt charged the pattern with magical powers,
and perhaps for this very reason appealed to primitive taste. Centuries earlier, Greek craftsmen had added a
number of Oriental animal figures to their antithetically placed pairs of animals on the gold plaque from
Vettersfelde (page 185). In the low relief on the gilded-silver phalera opposite, the creatures depicted are a

mixture of stereotyped realistic treatment and sheer fantasy. The fight at the center of the disk follows a Scythian model, but here is curiously distorted, with an unrecognizable predatory animal attacking from above, apparently for lack of space. On the other hand, the animals at the upper left are not fighting. The beast with its head turned back is an independent motif which derives from older Scythian work or some related Asiatic style. It serves to fill the space between the two winged animals, as does the bull's head on the opposite side between the two griffins.

Ornamental harness plaque (phalera). Gilded silver. From an unknown site on the Black Sea. Bibliothèque Nationale, Cabinet des Médailles, Paris

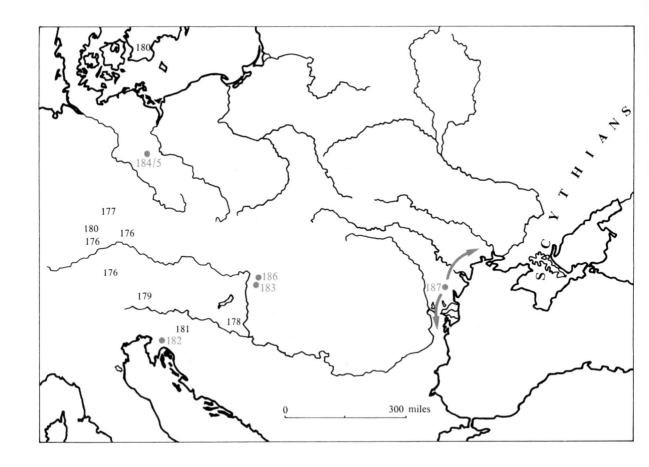

Sites with finds related to the early nomadic horsemen

Red: Scythian and Sarmatian finds or indigenous imitations.

Although the nomadic horsemen from the East played an important cultural role throughout Europe, the various regions involved were affected to very different degrees. Almost all the objects associated with these peoples that have been discovered in the West belong to the oldest stage of the Hallstatt period, but cannot be reliably assigned to any known group or people. Apart from a few artifacts, only the pictorial representations reflect the way of life of the nomadic horsemen. It appears that the newcomers became rapidly assimilated and soon gave up their own material culture, including such objects as horse-shaped clubs (p. 178). Scythian material culture and artistic forms had little influence and were only occasionally imitated in the West (p. 182). By contrast, a blend of traditional and alien elements gave rise in the Hallstatt epoch to a new style strikingly illustrated by the motif of the man on horseback. This motif became widespread and occurs even in the far North; the representations of mounted men from Järrestad (p. 180, top) are far from being as rare as might be inferred from this map. Similar rock drawings, incised designs on clay vessels, and embossed or repoussé figural ornamentation are also found elsewhere in southern Scandinavia and northeastern Germany. Sarmatian influence is negligible, since at this time Celtic styles prevailed in the West, while southeastern Europe and Sarmatian art were drawing on Greco-Scythian traditions.

Chronological chart of the early nomadic horsemen

The numbers refer to pages. The more thickly shaded areas indicate the absolute age of the finds in question. For chronology of the Hallstatt period, see p. 157; for that of the La Tène, p. 251.

This chart includes only those nomadic peoples for whom there is reliable archaeological or historical evidence and who are represented by illustrations in this book. During the second half of the eighth century B.C., sites in Central Europe testify to new developments. A new type of harness gear made its appearance, a type known to have existed earlier in the region north of the Black Sea. The westward diffusion of such finds reflects the wanderings of peoples from the East—a movement that was touched off by the Scythian invasion of Cimmerian settlements. One part of the Cimmerians moved to Asia Minor, while another was pushed into the Danube Valley. From here, the movement, which probably involved a number of different tribes, was gradually extended into South Germany and Central Italy. Connections with the East left their mark on what archaeologists call Hallstatt stage C, and brought about Central Europe's first contacts with Greek culture. Henceforward, the development of Central European culture is bound up with historical events on the northern boundary of the Mediterranean world. The Scythian incursions westward during the fifth century B.C. left no permanent mark. From the third century on, the Sarmatians and other races of mounted nomads achieved a dominant position around the Black Sea, which they maintained down to the period of the great migrations and the coming of the Goths.

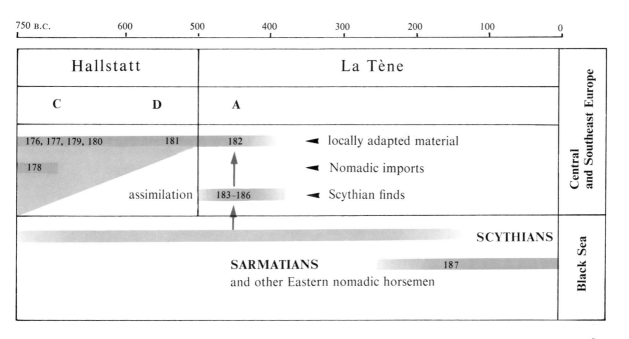

Statuette of a man with a weapon (?) on his shoulder. Bronze, height 1³/₄″. From the *oppidum* on the Hradiště, Stradonice, Bohemia, Czechoslovakia. National Museum, Prague

During the half-millennium preceding the birth of Christ, art in most parts of Prehistoric Europe came under predominantly Celtic influences. Close contacts with the Mediterranean world gave rise to entirely new styles almost independent of indigenous traditions. These styles contrast sharply with the geometric stiffness of the Hallstatt period. Human and animal figures are now conceived in a more realistic spirit, though the treatment is never crudely naturalistic. The statuette shown here may strike us as ungainly, but this is not due to any lack of skill on the part of the artist. Rather, it is because what he intended to represent does not require naturalistic treatment—it may even preclude it. The schematic human figure and the stylized birds on the belt hook from Hölzelsau (facing page) still derive from the Hallstatt repertory of motifs, whereas the volutes consisting of stylized animal bodies with heads at each end date from the middle of the La Tène period. But such stubborn clinging to old traditions in an especially conservative area like the Alps is merely the exception that proves the rule where the evolution of the La Tène style is concerned. It shows that certain ethnic groups were much slower than others to adjust to the forms introduced by Celtic newcomers. Apart from that, the La Tène style enables us to determine the extent of Celtic expansion only with the help of other archaeological evidence.

Belt hook (the ornamental openwork plaque was broken in Antiquity and reinforced with a bronze backing). Bronze, length 6³/₈″. From Hölzelsau, Kufstein, Tyrol, Austria. Prähistorische Staatssammlung, Munich

Fibula with mask (two views); spring and pin missing. Bronze, length ⁷/₈". From Schmidmühlen, Burglengenfeld, Bavaria, Germany. Prähistorische Staatssammlung, Munich

Fibula, showing in profile the head of a bird of prey, and from the front the head of a long-nosed fox. Bronze, length 1⁷/₈". From Kümmersbruck, Amberg, Bavaria, Germany. Prähistorische Staatssammlung, Munich

In the Early La Tène period, the most distinctive animal and human figures, though most often only heads, are to be found on bronze fibulae. The models were executed very carefully and cast by the lost-wax process. Among the animal figures, birds predominate, occasionally with fantastic profiles in total disregard of natural forms. The human faces nearly always look like masks and most often are set on the lower end of the fibula, projecting upward from the part that holds the pin so that they are turned toward the wearer. A large number of workshops supplied these pins, chiefly to a limited group of clients in the locality. In very small fibulae, the facial details are necessarily crudely executed, but certain features—for example, the prominent, almond-shaped eyes and the hair or headdress—are always carefully worked.

In a few masterly specimens, e.g., the fibula from Parsberg, eyeballs and nostrils are indicated, and the eyebrows are given special prominence. This particular
brooch is an exemplary model of decorative handling
determined by function. The two human heads are harmoniously adapted to the shape of the bow, while at the
bottom two mythical creatures, whose tails trace a single
volute design, form the catchplate. The artist here went
beyond Hallstatt schematization, helped by classical
suggestions but in an entirely unclassical way. The two
human heads, especially, have no counterpart in the
art of ancient Greece.

Fibula with masks and fantastic animals forming
the ornamental clasp. Bronze, length 3½". From
Parsberg, Bavaria, Germany. Germanisches
Nationalmuseum, Nuremberg

Finger rings with male and female figures. Bronze, height 1″. From Stuttgart-Uhlbach, Baden-Württemberg, Germany. Württembergisches Landesmuseum, Stuttgart

The symbolic significance of the pair of rings from Stuttgart-Uhlbach is clearly indicated by the male and female human figures. Where the human face and figure are transposed into pure ornament, this significance becomes blurred. In the ornamental wrought-copper sheaths from Tal-y-Llyn (facing page), the symmetrical faces are so completely subordinated to the simplified palmette ornamentation that they can scarcely be regarded as symbolizing two people. Even though the figures are extremely stylized, however, eyes and eyebrows are emphasized in the La Tène manner, and the small tight-lipped mouth is also characteristic (cf. page 240). In contrast, the almost demonic expression of the figure on the harness pin from Urach results from an exaggeration imposed by the size of the metal piece rather than from any attempt to create a demonic effect. The mask features with a hint of shoulders and arms remain in keeping with the object's function. In comparison with the mask, the tracery on the ornamental belt plaque from Stupava (facing page) seems too delicate, although it is obviously built around the mask at its center.

Front pin of an axle tree. Iron, width 3¹/₈″. From Urach, Reutlingen, Baden-Württemberg, Germany. Württembergisches Landesmuseum, Stuttgart

Ornamental belt plaque with low relief and engraving. Bronze, length 2³/₄″. From Stupava, Slovakia. Slovak National Museum, Bratislava

Decorated sheaths. Copper, length c. 6″ and c. 6³/₄″. From Tal-y-Llyn, Merionethshire, Wales. National Museum of Wales, Cardiff

Fibula with finely modeled sheep's head; pin missing. Length 3¹/₈″. From Panenský Týnec, Bohemia, Czechoslovakia. National Museum, Prague

Drinking-horn mount (detail). Sheet gold, length of the ram's head ⁵/₈″. From the royal grave at Kleinaspergle, Asperg, Ludwigsburg, Baden-Württemberg, Germany. Württembergisches Landesmuseum, Stuttgart

Drinking-horn mounts terminating in rams' heads. Embossed sheet gold, length c. 7″. From the royal grave at Kleinaspergle, near Asperg, Ludwigsburg, Baden-Württemberg, Germany. Württembergisches Landesmuseum, Stuttgart

Neck ring terminating in bulls' heads. Silver with iron core, greatest diameter $11^1/_2''$, width of ring $1^5/_8''$, weight almost 15 lbs. From Trichtingen, Rottweil, Baden-Württemberg, Germany. Württembergisches Landesmuseum, Stuttgart

It is not absolutely certain that the gold mounts for drinking horns from Kleinaspergle (facing page) are Celtic works. There are Russian counterparts, presumably fashioned by Greek craftsmen in the Black Sea area for barbarian princes in eastern Europe. Possibly these mounts are merely very skillful imitations. Be that as it may, the imbrication on one mount and the plait band on the other are Greek motifs. The unusually realistic representation of a sheep's head on the brooch from Panenský Týnec (facing page, top left) might have been influenced by work similar to the rams' heads on the horn mounts. This is also true of the bulls' heads on the silver neck ring from Trichtingen, which is of somewhat later date. The motif may refer to the object's function: it was probably a ritual implement or adorned the neck of a stele dedicated to some deity. Cows and sheep, and especially bulls and rams, played an important part in Celtic mythology, but one is seldom able to say what they stood for in particular works.

Attic red-figure kylix from the workshop of the so-called Amymone Painter. Athens, c. 450 B.C. The central scene shows a priestess at an altar. The thin gold appliqués were added later by a native craftsman and are only partially preserved. Terra cotta, diameter 6″. From the royal grave at Kleinaspergle, Asperg, Ludwigsburg, Baden-Württemberg, Germany. Württembergisches Landesmuseum, Stuttgart

How very different the Celtic conception of art was from the Greek is occasionally shown by alterations made to imported Greek ware. Such imports, needless to say, are found only in graves of the rich and powerful, such as the royal grave at Kleinaspergle. The elegant simplicity of Attic bowls apparently appealed less to Celtic taste than polymorphous ornament, and in the example shown here, native artists "improved" upon the original by adding thin appliqués of gold foil. Their delight in strongly articulated surfaces led eventually to total transformation of the Greek models. The palmette, for instance, was converted into an ornament of intricately twining vine leaves and stems. Ultimately, this ornament was broken up into its individual components and reassembled in abstract geometric plant forms, so that in some cases it is nearly impossible to say what is background and what superposed pattern (cf. also page 252).

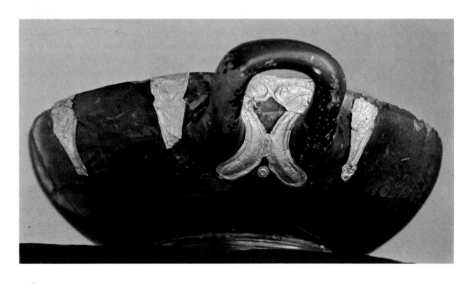

Outside of the kylix illustrated above

Ornamental openwork casing for a bowl (bowl reconstructed). Repoussé sheet gold, diameter 5″, height 3¼″. From Schwarzenbach, Birkenfeld, Rhineland-Palatinate, Germany. Antiquarium, Berlin

Repoussé ornamental plaque. Gold foil over iron backing, length 3$\frac{1}{8}$″, thickness of iron backing $\frac{3}{16}$″. From Weiskirchen, Merzig-Wadern, Saarland, Germany. Rheinisches Landesmuseum, Trier

The plant ornamentation of the Early La Tène period appears as something new primarily on account of its composition. Intrication of the basic pattern and complication of the motif are raised to the status of a principle in these two gold ornamental plaques. The painterly effect of the relief work is sometimes enhanced by coral inlays. Swirling rhythms and a balanced arrangement of the bladderlike patterns dissolve the entire surface into dynamic curves. Filigree decoration around undecorated areas brings out the deliberate intricacy of the ornamentation by breaking up the areas of reflected light. In such elaborate ornamentation, the stylized human faces would scarcely be noticed had they not been placed at central points.

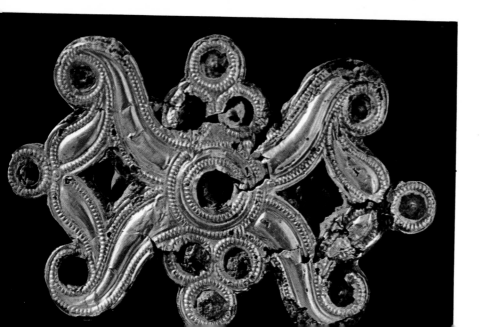

Repoussé ornamental plaque. Sheet gold with iron backing (originally, disks of coral were probably fastened with gold pegs in the thirteen beaded circles), length 2$\frac{3}{4}$″. From the royal grave at Kleinaspergle, Asperg, Ludwigsburg, Baden-Württemberg, Germany. Württembergisches Landesmuseum, Stuttgart

Ornamental disk. Repoussé sheet gold on bronze with filigree decoration and coral inlays. From Auvers-sur-Oise (Seine-et-Oise), France. Bibliothèque Nationale, Cabinet des Médailles, Paris

Flask with human legs. Repoussé sheet bronze with fine engraving in the circular ornamental field, height c. 19½", capacity 18½ quarts. From Dürrnberg, Hallein, Salzburg, Austria. Museum, Hallein

Long-spouted pitcher. Bronze, height 14⅝". From the royal grave at Kleinaspergle, Asperg, Ludwigsburg, Baden-Württemberg, Germany. Württembergisches Landesmuseum, Stuttgart
▼

That a prosperous upper class in the Early La Tène period adopted Mediterranean ways of life can best be inferred from the fact that it imported both wine and drinking vessels. Native craftsmen soon learned to imitate these, however, altering the ancient models in many ways and sometimes producing very large vessels. The wine flask from Hallein is a reproduction of the so-called pilgrims' bottles from Italy, designed (when of normal size) for easy carrying. The human-shaped legs may thus refer to the original use of such vessels.

Rim of the bronze pitcher from Kleinaspergle (facing page). The masklike human head is at the top of the handle. Width 3¼″

Handle appliqué of the bronze pitcher from Kleinaspergle (facing page). Height 2¾″

Wine jugs were first commissioned from Etruscan workshops which, in turn, made use of Greek models. In the imitations manufactured north of the Alps, the appliqué at the base of the handle turned into a sort of leaf motif arranged in layers, which has been transformed into a bladderlike pattern in our example from Kleinaspergle. At the same time, classical regresentations of faces or busts on the palmette handle attachments give way to the Early La Tène stylizations of human features. Here, the result is a peculiar hybrid, a kind of Celtic Silenus whose beard is divided in order to adapt to the palmette pattern. The mask on the rim of the pitcher is even more peculiar. The two prolongations of the handle juncture, which was formerly plain, were ordinarily shaped as crouching animals. Here, they seem to have become the outspread arms of the central mask.

Even before the La Tène period, the region around Hallstatt kept up close trade connections with northern Italy by way of the Alpine passes. This trade continued in the Early La Tène period, and it is not surprising, therefore, that pottery wine pitchers dating from that time look like copies of Italian models. The few painted specimens of such long-spouted pitchers similarly go back to ancient prototypes. They constitute links in a chain that hundreds of archaeological finds together confirm. Thanks to its link with Italy, the eastern Celtic region enjoyed the same cultural advantage over the Germanic North as did the West, which had easy access (via the Rhône) to the Greek colonies along the Mediterranean. Moreover, this region seems to have been

Long-spouted jug. Painted clay, height 16½″. From Hallstatt, Upper Austria. Museum, Hallstatt

more prosperous economically and better organized politically. The royal grave at Reinheim testifies to the wealth of individual princes who employed the best native craftsmen (cf. pages 208, 209). The flagon with a tubular spout (facing page) is one of the masterpieces of Early La Tène metalwork. It reflects Celtic standards in every feature of its design and decoration. Though the little horse on the lid was certainly derived from much older Greek models, its bearded human face is not that of a genuine centaur but of some hybrid Greek-Celtic fantasy animal. The two interlocking motifs on the upper part of the handle follow the same principle: the beard and cheeks of a human face are inserted between the horns of a ram's head, and what looks, from the side, like the tail of a palmette on the lid is actually part of the hairdress of the stylized human features.

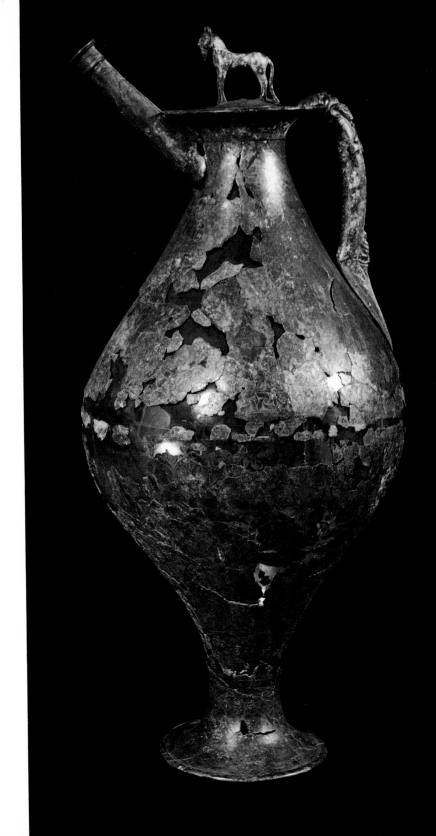

Flagon with tubular spout. (The figure on the lid is a horse with bearded human head.) Gilded and engraved sheet bronze, height 20¹/₄″, greatest width 9¹/₈″. From the royal grave at Reinheim, St. Ingbert, Saarland, Germany. Staatliches Museum für Vor- und Frühgeschichte, Saarbrücken

If the tiny statue of a boar from Balzers (below) served as a mounting on a helmet, its stylization may be accounted for by some intended magical effect. The essential physical features of the animal, including its great strength, are perfectly expressed in the flowing line from the elongated snout to the arched and bristling back, the big eyes, and the ears alert to danger. Large sculptures are often treated in a similar way: the figure as a whole being simplified, particular portions emphasized for visual effect, and natural proportions disregarded (cf. page 227). On the so-called sacrificial panel of the Gundestrup caldron (page 225), the foot soldiers wear plain helmets or more probably caps, while the leader of the group blowing horns at the right of the marching men wears, like one of the horsemen, a helmet decorated with the figure of a boar. Like the emblems of the Gauls, this obviously indicated membership of a specific group. As the emblem of a military or religious company, the animal figure may involve reference to some particular god—the boar-god Moccus, for instance —unless it had some kind of totemistic meaning and indicated members of a group bound by kinship ties.

Statuette of a boar, possibly from a helmet. Cast bronze, height 1⁵/₈″. From Balzers, Liechtenstein. Historical Collection, Vaduz

So-called lentiform bottle. Pottery with impressed patterns and engraved animal frieze on shoulder (cf. fig. 12), height 9⅜". From Matzhausen, Burglengenfeld, Bavaria, Germany. Museum für Vor- und Frühgeschichte, Berlin

The introduction of the potter's wheel north of the Alps early in the La Tène period led at once to experiments with ceramic form. The new device led to the production of such unusual shapes as the so-called lentiform bottles characterized by round, flat bodies. The bottle from Matzhausen also has a rather rare animal frieze, the motifs employed harking back to a period prior to the wheel. Stags, does, boars, and great capercaillies are invariably represented in pairs, and, in addition, there is a dog or wolf pursuing a hare. The animal bodies are articulated in terms of ornament: for instance, the legs are assimilated to the usual bladderlike pattern. The motifs go back to painted friezes on pottery pitchers from Rhodes or Corinth dating from the seventh century B.C. Similar friezes survive in situla art (cf. page 143). The use of such old prototypes is characteristic of La Tène art: it preserves traditional classical elements down to the very end of the period, but stylizes them in its own way (cf. page 208).

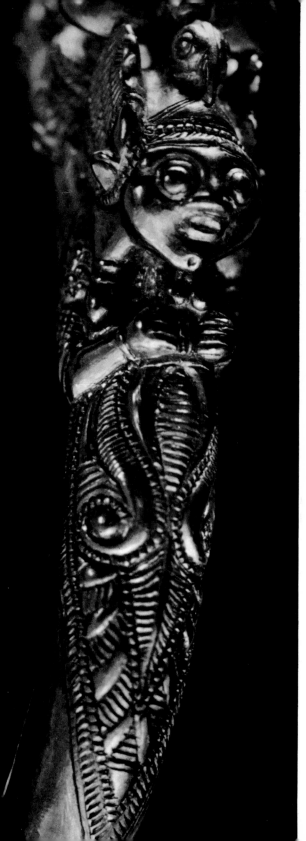

Detail of the bracelet from the royal grave at Reinheim (see facing page), showing a bird perched on top of a human figure (indicated only by its head and arms). Gold, height of head with bird $^1/_2''$. Staatliches Museum für Vor- und Frühgeschichte, Saarbrücken

The Rhineland Celts of the Early La Tène period were particularly skillful in organically combining figural motifs and ornamentation. Some gold neck rings and bracelets, such as those from Reinheim (facing page), are notable cases in point. They terminate in knobs, beneath which small lions' heads are set at either side. Between the terminal knob and the twisted torque of the neck ring is a modeled human head wearing a helmet shaped like a bird. A neck ornament with three tassels supplies the link between the face and the torque itself. The combination of motifs is repeated on the bracelet, but here the human figure is shown down to the arms. From the arms, the ornamental area extends onto the ring of the bracelet, like a continuation of the costume, where it narrows down to a point. There can be no doubt that this was the work of a master familiar with Greek models, as can be seen in the imbricated motif which seems to indicate the sleeves of the figure. As a whole, the composition goes back to such a sculptured scene as we find on at least one hydria (water jar) from Grächwyl, dating from the Hallstatt period. This shows a winged female figure standing between two lions, with a hare in front of her and a large bird with powerful wings above her. On the objects from Reinheim, this bird was mistakenly represented as a helmet, and all that remains of the lions are the leonine masks on either side of the terminals. The hare or rabbit is missing in the later work, but the wings of the bird may have survived as the suggestion of scales over the sleeves. Thus, some Greek or Etruscan scene which probably showed a Mistress of the Beasts—perhaps Artemis—was transposed into a motif which preserves hardly anything of its original meaning. Here, as elsewhere, an old Hallstatt motif inspired a new La Tène creation (cf. page 207).

Neck ring and bracelet, both hollow, with similar repoussé ornaments at the terminals. Gold, greatest diameter of the torque 6″, of the bracelet 2³/₈″. From the royal grave at Reinheim, St. Ingbert, Saarland, Germany. Staatliches Museum für Vor- und Frühgeschichte, Saarbrücken

As insignia of gods or persons of high rank, perhaps also as warriors' decorations, the La Tène necklets reflect the general evolution of style but are often set apart by extremely elaborate treatment. The bronze neck ring from Montans (page 211) marks a second stylistic stage on the European Continent, the so-called mature, or Waldalgesheim, style. The work is pleasing, combining as it does a well-proportioned shape with a delicate spiral decoration. The Celts of the islands often came up with solutions of their own to traditional problems (cf. pages 210, 211). Their repoussé work in laminated gold is distinguished by elegant line, complete mastery of ornamental design, and workmanship that gives the impression of casual effortlessness although it rests upon careful planning.

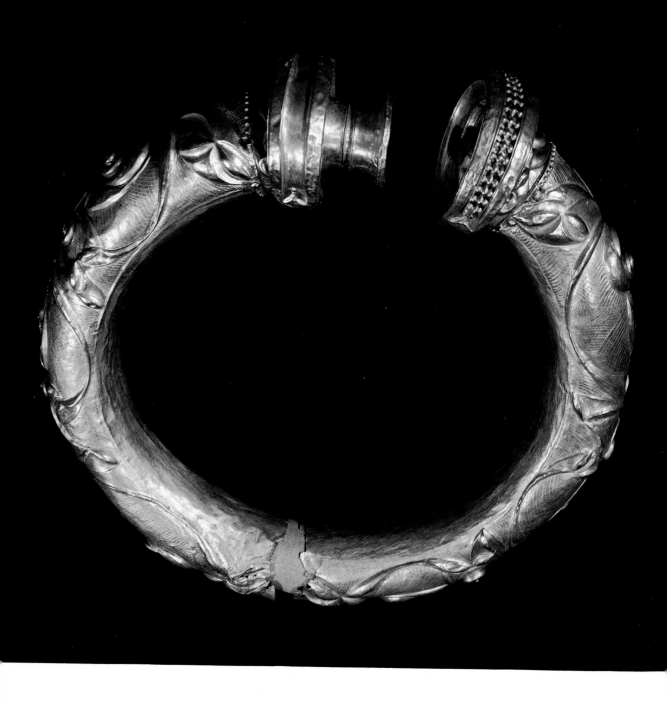

Neck ring with socketed clasp. Repoussé sheet gold, inside diameter c. 8¹/₂″. From a hoard of gold objects at Broighter, Limavady, County Londonderry, Ireland. National Museum, Dublin

210

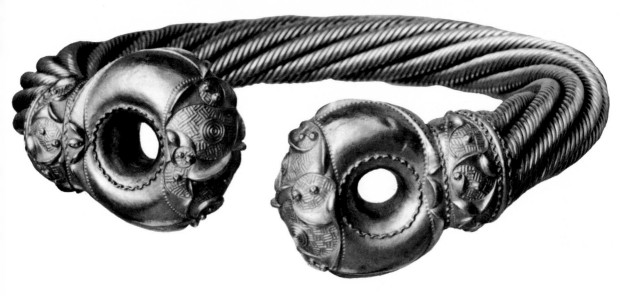

Torque of twisted wire with repoussé-decorated hollow pierced knobs at either end. Electrum, diameter 7³/₄″. From a gold hoard at Snettisham, Norfolk, England. British Museum, London

Neck ring with "buffer" terminals (detail). Cast bronze, diameter 5″. From Montans (Tarn), France. Musée des Antiquités Nationales, Saint-Germain-en-Laye

Two fibulae linked by a chain with small tin pendants. Bronze with red enamel inlays, length of fibulae $3^1/_4''$. From Campi Neri (Nonsberg-Cles), South Tyrol, Italy. Prähistorische Staatssammlung, Munich

Among objects of everyday use, the most frequent decorated pieces are items of female attire. Fibulae, especially, are often both utilitarian and attractive, though not necessarily elaborate. In some cases, the decorative element is no more than a chain suspended from two fibulae and hung with small pieces of tin. Often, coral or enamel inlays enhance the unpretentious forms. To appreciate the original color effect, one must imagine the contrast between the glint of the bronze when it was new and the white or red inlays. That the fibulae are so often found in pairs is accounted for by practical necessity: wrap-around shawls have to be pinned at the shoulders or at either side of the bosom. The graves of well-to-do women contain large numbers of fibulae, the popularity of which went beyond their utilitarian functions. They had a traditional symbolic meaning as amulets. Pins and fibulae, left as votive gifts or thank offerings for good health or fertility, were deposited over more than a thousand years in natural shrines and temples from Greece to western Europe: graves like those at Campi Neri are typical.

Miniature dog (two views). Colored glass, length $^3/_4''$. From Wallertheim, Alzey, Rhineland-Palatinate, Germany. Museum, Alzey

Many objects which were made of organic materials and then painted have disappeared forever. The painted pottery that has come down to us preserves but a small fraction of the colors actually used in Prehistoric times. Because the metalwork survives best, we are likely to think of Prehistoric art as more or less monochrome. Just how lively the colors were in the La Tène period can perhaps best be seen from the multicolored glass ornaments. Like the fibulae, these were primarily articles of feminine apparel. From the Middle La Tène period on, glass bracelets became increasingly fashionable, and beads occur in many shapes and colors. In this category, the so-called eye beads (either made or painted to look like eyes) had a pronounced magical character; they served to ward off evil powers. Men wore them also for this purpose and occasionally left them as offerings in caves. Glass figurines like the little dog from Wallertheim are rare. It may have been a real *objet de luxe,* for figures of dogs are infrequently found in the La Tène period, even though—or perhaps because—they were kept in large numbers. The body of the dog consists of opaque blue glass overlaid with white and yellow stripes. The La Tène period's predilection for these three colors is probably accounted for by technical reasons. Opaque glass is easier to manufacture than transparent glass such as was used, for instance, in the more elaborate bracelets.

Jewelry. Colored glass, diameter of bracelet (bottom left) c. $3^1/_2''$. From Baden-Württemberg, Germany. Württembergisches Landesmuseum, Stuttgart

Jar. Painted clay, height 14⁵/₈″. From a site near the gasworks, Basel, Switzerland. Historisches Museum, Basel

Jar. Painted clay, height 11½″. From the *oppidum* at Manching, Ingolstadt, Bavaria, Germany. Prähistorische Staatssammlung, Munich

Jar. Painted clay, height 11″. From the *oppidum* at Manching, Ingolstadt, Bavaria, Germany. Prähistorische Staatssammlung, Munich

▼

Toward the close of the La Tène period, a city culture made its appearance in the lands of the eastern Celts, though it was confined to large fortified places, the so-called *oppida*. Under ancient Mediterranean influences, these towns became seats of government, and probably also contained the dwellings of the nobility. At the same time, they probably functioned as centers of trade and worship, and we know that a few were important manufacturing sites. Recent excavations at Manching have shown that coins were minted there (cf. page 217), and many consumer goods were produced in large quantities, including painted pottery, all of which was made with the aid of a wheel. The delicately colored patterns reflect local taste and workshop traditions: even in nearby Switzerland quite different shapes and ornaments were favored.

Celtic coin of the Parisii with stylized portrait of Philip II of Macedon. Gold, diameter 1$^{1}/_{8}$″. Bibliothèque Nationale, Cabinet des Médailles, Paris

Bavarian Celtic coins. Upper row gold, lower row silver, diameter $^1/_2$–$^5/_8$″. Upper row, from left to right: from Oberübermoos, Wasserburg; from Upper Bavaria; and from Irsching, Pfaffenhofen an der Ilm. Lower row: from the Manching *oppidum*, Ingolstadt; and from Bucherforst, Hinterpfeinach, Uffenheim. Prähistorische Staatssammlung, Munich

More emphatically than any other relics, Celtic coins point to Mediterranean influences. Trade in kind gave way gradually to more developed forms of exchange. This began in Gaul, when coins from the Greek colonies became the accepted currency. To mint coins, however, presupposes a master of the mint and hence political entities that did not arise in the eastern Celtic regions until a relatively late date. Discoveries at the Manching *oppidum* include clay molds for casting small gold disks. These disks were then stamped with an iron seal, and thus converted into the coins known in Germany as "little rainbow bowls" (upper row, above). The symbols on the coins do not denote definite values, but rather the place where the coins were minted and, by the same token, an area occupied by a given tribe. Coins of this kind, however, circulated outside the area where they were minted, their value being determined by their gold or silver content. Except for purely symbolic signs, such as sun, moon, or bird's head, the images stamped on the coins go back to Greek prototypes. Thus, the Parisii, probably as early as the third century B.C., minted a gold coin showing the head of Philip II of Macedon (359–336 B.C.), but the copy is very different from the original. The gold stater of Philip showed, on one side, a laurel-wreathed head of Apollo; in the Celtic imitation, the Hellenistic hairstyle is replaced by a pattern of curves and spirals (facing page), and the face is broken up by swirls into separate fields. According to Caesar, the Celtic populations were familiar with the Greek language and script. This no doubt explains why, instead of taking Roman coins as their models, they favored those used in the Greek colonies closer to them.

In the Germanic North, which had no direct contact with the Mediterranean world, the arts and crafts took part in the over-all European development only marginally and indirectly, through the Celts. The relatively low economic level and type of social organization prevalent in this region had much to do with this development, or lack of it. It is interesting to note that such objects as were imported from elsewhere were not luxury articles but, in the main, ritual objects, such as caldrons (which were more or less common property, cf. page 225). The Dejbjerg wagon, shown here, probably falls into this category: the thronelike seat at the center would seem to be intended for a dignitary, if not for a deity. It is very possible that it was for the fertility goddess Nerthus. Tacitus mentions that, every year, the statue of the goddess was taken in a carriage to a lake, where it was washed. Celtic cartwrights enjoyed a high reputation even in Rome, but the provenance of our example cannot be ascertained. The bronze fittings are late works, done when the Celtic style had become stereotyped, but they might very well have been executed by Germanic craftsmen raised in the Celtic tradition. The conjecture is at least plausible, in view of the many trade and cultural contacts between Germans and Celts in the Late La Tène period.

Ritual wagon (reconstructed) with ornamental bronze fittings (see facing page). Height c. 35″. Found in pieces in a bog at Dejbjerg, Ringkøbing, Jutland, Denmark. Nationalmuseet, Copenhagen

Celtic arms and armor, when employed as symbols of rank, were always lavishly decorated. Most of the helmets that have come down to us, a number of which are from wagon burials (cf. pages 206, 225), seem to be of this type. The helmet from Amfreville is decorated with a variety of scroll patterns in addition to an encircling gold band. Like it, the bronze ceremonial shields with glass or enamel inlays probably belonged to high-ranking warriors. On the shield found in the Thames (facing page), the repoussé pattern, consisting of three circles with small circles inside them, fits neatly into the shape of the shield. The division of the surface is here achieved with a few lines, but the stylization is of a pronouncedly Late British type: the Continent was too strongly influenced by Roman patterns ever to develop anything like this.

Ceremonial shield. Repoussé bronze with red glass inlays, height 31$\frac{1}{2}$". From the Thames at Battersea, London, England. British Museum, London

◄ Ceremonial helmet. Bronze sheathed in sheet iron with enamel ornamentation and a gold band around the middle, height 6$\frac{1}{4}$". From Amfreville-sous-les-Monts (Eure), France. The Louvre, Paris

In the first century B.C., the island Celts attained undisputed mastery in the decoration of flat surfaces. What might at first glance appear as sheer fantasy is actually the result of deliberate composition, though the traditional motifs are transformed in a characteristic way. The decorated side of the mirror from Desborough takes the swelling volutes and bladder patterns of La Tène art and refines them to the point of geometric stylization. In delicate arabesques, they are carefully subordinated to the basic over-all design, which is adapted to the shape of the mirror. Embossed work on three-dimensional pieces is executed with the same gracefulness and the same sense of proportion. The pattern on the bronze "Petrie Horns," presumably a crown (facing page), is no less well adapted to the austere shape of the object. Ornamentation is most effective where its own basic structure brings out the shape of an object. This purpose is achieved to perfection through the off-center design on the bronze bowl from an unknown site in Ireland (page 224): bowl and decoration are in perfect balance.

Parts of what is presumed to have been a crown, known as the "Petrie Horns." Bronze, maximum height 3⁷/₈″, width c. 4″. From an unknown site in Ireland. National Museum, Dublin

Bowl with wide rim in repoussé. Bronze, diameter c. 10″.
From an unknown site in Ireland. British Museum, London

Ritual caldron made of several separate plates fastened together. Seven of the original eight outer plates are preserved; of the six ▶
inner plates, five run around the wall of the vessel and one is on the bottom. Silvered copper with traces of gold leaf on the figurative work and remnants of glass paste in the eyes of the figures, diameter across the rim 27″. From Gundestrup, Amt Aalborg,
Jutland, Denmark. Nationalmuseet, Copenhagen

The age and provenance of the silver caldron from Gundestrup have been variously estimated. Judging by the character of the decoration, however, there is good reason to believe that it was produced in northern Gaul in the first century B.C. The elements borrowed from Mediterranean motifs once again illustrate the fact that La Tène craftsmen made use of very old models. Celtic and predominantly Greek ideas are blended here, probably having lost a great deal of their original meaning. The conception of a stag-god, for instance, is Celtic, but the representation of such a god holding a stag in each upraised hand follows Mediterranean models. On one of the inside plates, the same god, Cernunnos, this time with antlers on his head, is shown with legs crossed in the Celtic manner (cf. page 243) beside a stag. Another inside plate (visible in the photograph) depicts Celtic costumes and weapons with great accuracy, as we can tell from other archaeological finds as well as from historical accounts. However, the leafy staff between the soldiers on horse and those on foot is borrowed from much older Mediterranean vase paintings. The most recent interpretation of the staff as a ritual pole is based on the positivist assumption that Prehistoric pictorial sequences always depicted a real event and must have had a tangible meaning for the artists and their contemporaries. But just as the Gundestrup silversmiths could never have seen the fantastic creatures they depicted, so their works cannot invariably be interpreted as mere records of either real or mythical events.

Stag with movable antlers. Cast bronze, height 13³/₄″. From a hoard at Neuvy-en-Sullias (Loiret), France. Musée Historique de l'Orléanais, Orléans

Boar with stylized bristles. Bronze, ▶ height 27″. From a hoard at Neuvy-en-Sullias (Loiret), France. Musée Historique de l'Orléanais, Orléans

The fact that Celtic art tends to avoid realism in treating animal figures has been explained, among other things, as being due to a religious taboo against the literal rendering of natural forms. In addition, many deities were represented as specific animal species or were closely associated with them. There is no need, however, to attribute this particular mode of representing animals to the awe inspired by a divine image. Quite apart from all symbolic content, figural representation is subject to the same radical stylization as ornament: it seems hardly possible that two completely unlike tendencies should develop simultaneously in any art. That is why, in profile, the boar from Neuvy-en-Sullias is almost pure ornament, appearing to be mainly composed of two large bladderlike surfaces. All the same, the stylized figure most convincingly renders the animal's basic characteristics (cf. page 206).

Horse with remnant of a bit in its mouth. Bronze, length $4^3/_4''$. From a grave containing a wagon at Freisen, St. Wendel, Saarland, Germany. Rheinisches Landesmuseum, Trier

The legs of the little horse from Freisen, which has the appearance of a stereotyped statuette, are rendered naturalistically, but head and neck are stylized out of their natural proportions. In objects of everyday use with figural decoration, the simplification of natural forms and their reduction to bare essentials is carried to its utmost. In the yoke mount from Manching (facing page) the bovine and bird heads are no more than terminals for the U-shaped volutes which, in themselves, as it were, fulfill the practical purpose of rein guides as well as the aesthetic one of ornamentation. Certain animal and human figures in bronze, on the other hand, such as the crude ones from Campi Neri (facing page), exhibit no artistic qualities whatever. They were massproduced devotional objects and their symbolic content was all that mattered.

Yoke fitting with stylized bird and bovine heads. Bronze, height 3½″. From the *oppidum* at Manching, Ingolstadt, Bavaria, Germany. Prähistorische Staatssammlung, Munich

Three human figures and a horse. Sheet bronze with punched patterns, length of horse 2⅜″, height of human figures 2⅛″–2⅜″. From Campi Neri (Nonsberg-Cles), South Tyrol, Italy. Prähistorische Staatssammlung, Munich

By contrast with the *oppida,* which were political and economic centers, countless Celtic sanctuaries, large and small, show that religion played a large part in the public life of these people. Especially in Gaul, they attest to the existence of a priesthood, the Druids. Temples like Roquepertuse, which is decorated with magnificent sculptures, were the objects of pilgrimage from distant lands (cf. pages 241, 247). Smaller places were celebrated for the healing virtues of their wells (cf. page 234). Many of these old shrines were destroyed in Roman times, but here and there the old worship survived, under new names, even in Christian times. In a number of localities, buried hoards are the only testimony to the existence of these Prehistoric shrines (cf. page 244).

Aerial photograph of rectangular entrenchment at Buchenberg, Starnberg, Bavaria, Germany. This site of an old Celtic place of worship measures approximately 115 × 130 yards

Ritual statuettes. Left: ram; cast bronze, height $2^1/_8''$; from Sempt, Ebersberg, Bavaria, Germany. Right: bull; cast bronze, height $2^7/_8''$; from Weltenburg, Kelheim, Bavaria, Germany. Prähistorische Staatssammlung, Munich

Under the influence of Roman cults, religious architecture developed into the Gallo-Roman peripteral temple of stone or wood. In the Celtic parts of Europe, as yet unoccupied by the Romans, there was the parallel development of quadrangular entrenchments during the Late La Tène period (facing page). Although they occur only in certain areas of southern Germany and Normandy, they share some features with Gaulish religious structures, such as shafts in which offerings were deposited. There are also remains of structures without the archaeological evidence beneath them which we would expect to find under secular buildings. Finally, the quadrangular walls around the sites, which probably replaced earlier wooden fences, are not to be mistaken for some sort of military defense. Rather, the regular shape served to set them apart from the profane world around them. The approximately square ground plan (usually measuring about eighty to a hundred yards each way) can be accounted for only by the fact that sacred structures had to conform to strict specifications. In the neighborhood of such places, little bronze sculptures, which obviously played a part in the rites, have occasionally been discovered. The ram from Sempt shown here, for example, brings to mind the processions of rams that were still held in many localities down to modern times.

Votive boat with separately modeled figure of an
oarsman. Clay, length of boat 4″, height (with figure)
2¹/₂″. From Magdalensberg, Klagenfurt, Carinthia,
Austria. Landesmuseum für Kärnten, Klagenfurt

Votive boat. Engraved and painted sheet bronze (the ▶
figure cast in bronze), length of boat 13¹/₂″, greatest
width 6³/₄″. From the Gallo-Roman cemetery at Blessey
(Côte d'Or), France. Musée Archéologique, Dijon

Prominent in Celtic art are human figures in mythical contexts. The meaning of the motifs cannot always be deciphered, and in some cases it is necessary to look far afield for a clue. The primitive clay sculpture of a man in a boat from Magdalensberg rests on the belief that the dead are conveyed over water to a life after death (cf. page 148). The same idea is rendered more skillfully in bronze sculptures from sanctuaries in Gaul. The one from Blessey, for example, is unmistakably derived from a Roman prototype. The unassuming clay sculpture from Magdalensberg (facing page) probably derives from older Italic models. Both sculptures reflect a Celtic conception of the afterworld which survived well into the Middle Ages. As late as the eleventh or twelfth century A.D., nobles and members of the clergy alike still placed the dead in boats or coffins waterproofed with tar and launched them at the mouth of the Rhône, from where they were supposed to travel to the Elysian Fields. To this day, the Irish say of someone who has just died: "He sailed yesterday; he had a good crossing."

Votive figures. Wood, height of statue 22⁷/₈″, of head 8⁵/₈″. From a well at the sanctuary of Montbouy (Loiret), France. Musée Historique de l'Orléanais, Orléans

The wells and ponds belonging to places of worship were regarded as links with the gods of the underworld. Occasionally, offerings and votive gifts are found in them. Apparently, Christian zealots, bent on wiping out paganism, often threw temple sculptures into water as one way of blotting out its very memory. In the wooden sculptures shown here, the human figure is reduced to the simple formula characteristic of ritual poles, and the heads have no more than the indications of eyes, nose, and mouth. On this score, the figures exhibit remarkable formal affinities with the stele from Stockach, which may be similarly conceived of as an individual likeness (see page 134). Such offerings were probably made in the hope of receiving good health or some other blessing, or as thank offerings.

The name inscribed upon it distinguishes the statue shown here from every other treatment of the human figure in Prehistoric art. As a work of art, it is insignificant. Like others of its kind, it takes us back to the vast category of pole sculptures, and for this reason has been regarded as the last of the menhirs. Probably dating from the first century B.C., the head clearly discloses Roman influences. It is no surprise to find it in the eastern Alps, where a Celtic kingdom of Noricum was mentioned as an ally of Rome as early as 129 B.C. The face lacks all typically Celtic stylistic features, yet also fails to come up to the individuality of Roman portraiture. The column is more impressive than the head: it was obviously intended, in keeping with primitive logic, to call attention to the importance of the man portrayed.

Popaius Senator, head of an old man set on a pillar. Chlorite slate, height c. 10′. In the village square at Bichl, Matrei, Tyrol, Austria

Celtic stone carvings are not very numerous and are normally strongly influenced by Roman sculpture, particularly in Gaul. Those uninfluenced by Roman art are stylized in the manner of the small bronze sculptures. The head from a stele found at Heidelberg, for example, is treated purely in terms of ornament and exhibits the usual basic patterns: even the eyes look like part of a plant pattern. The design on the forehead is hard to interpret; the lower part, at least, stands for the eyebrows, a feature commonly emphasized. The large cushionlike bulges may suggest a particular way of dressing the hair, as on the stele from Pfalzfeld (cf. also pages 238, 240, 241). There is a face on the back of the head as well, even more pronouncedly stylized. The hairdress on the figure on the facing page may go back to Hellenistic influences, but the rest of the features are distinctly Celtic.

Fragmentary head from a life-sized stele. Red sandstone, height 11³/₄″. From Heidelberg, Baden-Württemberg, Germany. Badisches Landesmuseum, Karlsruhe

Head of a man wearing a neck ring. Argillaceous slate, height 9¼″. Found together with bones of sacrificed animals in a sacred enclosure at Mšecké-Žehrovice, Slaný, Czechoslovakia. National Museum, Prague

There is no articulation whatever of the egg-shaped face. Mustache and eyebrows have become spiral ornaments, and the protruding eyes are strongly outlined. Only the neck ring is rendered naturalistically, as can be seen by a comparison with that illustrated at the foot of page 211. Just what function these heads served is uncertain. The find from Heidelberg, at any rate, was part of a Janus-faced stele (cf. page 240), but the sculpture above may represent a god or a dignitary, and undoubtedly stood in a sanctuary (cf. page 239). Here, too, post-Celtic iconoclasts may have been responsible for the head having been broken off and thrown into a ditch.

All four sides of the pyramidal column from Pfalz-feld are covered with crude ornamentation surrounding a human face. The latter is in every case adapted to the curvilinear pattern by the stylized treatment of a neck ornament with three pendants, like that worn by the figures on the terminals of the neck ring from Reinheim (page 209), and by cushion- or bladderlike bulges over the head. They obviously represent the same motif as do the hornlike headdress on the Janiform statue from Holzgerlingen (page 240) and the similarly two-faced head from Roquepertuse (page 241). Both the bulges and the horn-shaped forms have been interpreted as birds' heads, but birds' wings would be more plausible. If they were wings, the relief from Pfalzfeld would echo the motifs on the gold rings from Reinheim, although the finds from Roquepertuse point to a different symbolism (see page 240). At all events, this is about as far as we can go in attempting to interpret these steles. Nor does the small sculpture from Euffigneix (facing page) with the figure of a boar on its chest help much. It is usually taken to be a god of the hunt or a boar-deity. However, we have seen (page 206) that the figure of a boar on a helmet could serve as an emblem of a specific social group, and the same emblem might well have been placed on the chest or elsewhere. Where essential parts of the sculpture are missing, as in the stele from Waldenbuch (facing page), interpretation breaks down entirely. The unworked lower part of this nearly square column was sunk into the ground. The verticals above the peculiarly stiff ornamentation may suggest a garment, as on one of the figures from Roquepertuse (page 242); and above these lines, the left arm has been preserved. This figure, too, seems to have grown out of the stone block, but unlike the Janiform steles, there is no corresponding right arm on the back (cf. page 240).

Pyramid with reliefs on all sides of a human head surrounded by ornamental motifs (the top is missing). Variegated sandstone, height $58^{1}/_{4}''$. From Pfalzfeld, St. Goar, Rhineland-Palatinate, Germany. Rheinisches Landesmuseum, Bonn

Male figure with neck ring and boar in relief on his chest. Limestone, height 10¼". From Euffigneix (Haute-Marne), France. Museum, Chaumont

▲
Lower part of a stele with decoration in low relief on all sides; part of an arm and hand survive on the front. Sandstone, height 49¼". Probably from Waldenbuch, Böblingen, Baden-Württemberg, Germany. Württembergisches Landesmuseum, Stuttgart

The stele from Holzgerlingen is in many respects a typical Celtic stone sculpture. Its most prominent characteristic is its resemblance to a column—a type of treatment long since abandoned, as we saw in the case of the monument from Hirschlanden (page 135). The shape is obviously appropriate, for in its double-sided, Janus-like quality, it represents an age-old mythical figure whose human features are only superficial characteristics. The arms are executed in crude relief, one on the front, the other on the back. The two faces are almost devoid of expression: mouth, eyes, and nose are suggested by the simplest lines, and the head is hairless. This last-mentioned detail represents a departure from the customary schema, and may have something to do with the figure's symbolic meaning. The impression of severity or austerity, however, may not have been intended, although it would be perfectly in keeping with the symbolism. Standing stiff and motionless, the figure looks out upon two worlds, the here-and-now and the beyond. That they should be linked is typical of Prehistoric thought. Whether the figure stands for a god or a demigod, or perhaps for some leader among the dead recognizable by name, is not relevant here. In any case, it is no accident that an even more impressive Janus figure decorated the portico of the sanctuary at Roquepertuse (facing page). In this center of Celtic worship we should expect to find outstanding works by the best crafts-

Janiform stele with one arm on each side. Sandstone, height 90$^1/_2$″. From Holzgerlingen, Böblingen, Baden-Württemberg, Germany. Württembergisches Landesmuseum, Stuttgart

Janiform head. Limestone with traces of paint (cf. page 247), height 7⁷/₈″. From the portico of the sanctuary at Roquepertuse (Bouches-du-Rhône), France. Musée d'Archéologie, Château Borély, Marseilles

men, and the fact that here, too, the two-faced head is extremely stylized can only be accounted for by the artist's conscious intention. The systematic exaggeration here is peculiarly lifeless: the stiffness of the treatment has become a stylistic device. The bald head and sharply outlined nose, eyes, mouth, and chin endow the sculpture with an expression of utter grimness—an expression that the maker of the statue from Holzgerlingen attempted to achieve by the same means of extreme simplification. The difference in quality between the two reflects varying degrees of closeness to classical Antiquity, but in both sculptures, the basic Celtic motif is identical down to the smallest detail. The peculiar forms that separate the two faces are very similar in both works, and if they are intended to convey the head or wings of a bird, then we must recognize that they belong to the bird of death, a gigantic stone sculpture of which hovered over the portico of the sanctuary at Roquepertuse. Below the latter, the skulls of slain enemies were placed in hollowed-out portions of the column.

Statue of a god or hero, apparently wearing a kind of leather coat; head missing. Limestone with traces of paint, height 41³/₈″. From the sanctuary at Roquepertuse (Bouches-du-Rhône), France. Musée d'Archéologie, Château Borély, Marseilles

The God of Bouray. Statue originally consisting of six plates; two tubular pieces (the arms) are missing; body and legs consist of two repoussé plates, one front and one back; the head is composed of two cast plates; one of the colored glass eyes survives; the legs terminate in a stag's hoofs. Copper, height 16¹/₂″. From the Juine at La Ferté-Alais, Bouray-sur-Juine (Seine-et-Oise), France. Musée des Antiquités Nationales, Saint-Germain-en-Laye

There are many representations of the Celtic gods and they exhibit a good deal of variation from one area to another; but the one found most frequently in Gaul is the stag-god Cernunnos. This may be connected with the sacrifice of a stag which, in classical times, was often linked with fertility and burial rites. The Celtic religions, however, were characterized by a peculiar nature mysticism which raised many animals to a mythical status, though this is not disclosed by the way they are represented. The movable antlers of the stag from Neuvy-en-Sullias (page 226) might suggest such an interpretation. Moreover, creatures half-human and half-animal figure largely, though just how we are to interpret them remains uncertain because the motifs are superabundant and there are many gaps both in archaeological and in written records. In any case, Cernunnos seems to have been especially worshiped in Gaul. Characteristic of this god is the fact that he is usually seen sitting with crossed legs, as is shown by two stone sculptures from Roquepertuse. Occasionally he is represented with antlers (cf. page 225), and his statue from Bouray-sur-Juine (facing page) has a stag's hoofs. This bronze sculpture is noteworthy because it reflects an attempt to combine traditional Celtic conceptions with Roman stylistic features. This is especially evident in the treatment of the face and hair. The old bladderlike ornament is still discernible in the hair, which is dressed in the Roman manner.

It is hard to decide whether Celtic sculptors merely clung to their own stylistic forms during the Gallo-Roman period, or whether they were simply not skillful enough, technically or artistically, to assimilate Greco-Roman art. However that may be, Celtic works sometimes exhibit a unique beauty for the very reason that they reflect two different artistic conceptions which a given master was free to combine in his own way. The dancer from Neuvy-en-Sullias is only remotely reminiscent of the expressiveness of Greco-Roman statuettes. Her limbs appear disjointed, their proportions distorted, and her stance is at once stiff and uncertain. And yet she has a grace all her own, which probably results from the artist's attempt to bring the classical prototype into line with Celtic conceptions. The indigenous tradition asserts itself as a rejection of naturalism. The animated figure has been approached by means of formulas; details are simplified. Here, we have echoes of the statuesque, ornamental

Statuette of a dancer. Cast bronze, height $5^1/_2''$. From a hoard at Neuvy-en-Sullias (Loiret), France. Musée Historique de l'Orléanais, Orléans

Mask. Repoussé sheet bronze, the eyes probably originally colored glass or enamel, height 6⁷/₈″. From an unknown site in the Pyrenees. Museum, Tarbes

treatment which had been carried to extremes long since, as in the mask from the Pyrenees, shown above. All the elements of the face are broken down into elementary geometric forms and then reassembled with complete disregard for nature.

In the Janiform head from Roquepertuse (facing page), the human image has been reduced to a schema and entirely transformed into the reflection of an idea. By Celtic standards, form and content are harmoniously balanced here (see also page 241). By contrast, the iron mask from Alençon seems, at first glance, to be naturalistic in expression. The irregularity of the features, including the way the mouth is shaped, might affect us more deeply if only the treatment reflected some conscious intention. But this can hardly be the case, for it would have been in contradiction to every rule. The apparent exception is probably accounted for by the material used and the technique: wrought iron is less pliable than stone and must be treated differently. Moreover, as the mask was found in the treasury of a place of worship, it must have served as a symbol rather than as a portrait. This is why its design is as conventionalized as that of the head from Roquepertuse. What at first glimpse might appear to be a departure from formula is, in fact, due to a lack of ability. Shortcomings of this kind reveal possibilities which Celtic sculpture never exploited.

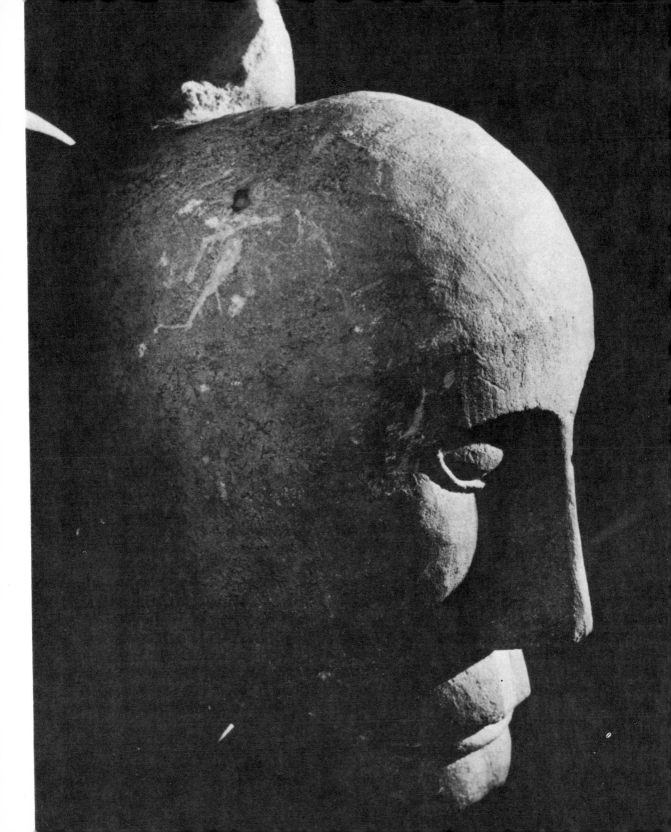

Head from a life-size statue of a man. Limestone with traces of red coloring, height 8″. From Gloucester, England. City Museum, Gloucester

Schematized human figure with mask features on ▶ the handle of a bowl. Bronze with enamel inlays. Irish work, eighth or ninth century A.D. From a Viking burial mound at Myklebostad, Eid, Norway. Museum, Bergen

Even during the Roman occupation, Celtic sculpture continued to go its own way in the British Isles, for all its exposure to classical models. The life-size statue from Gloucester is obviously based on classical monuments, though only the hairstyle is a true imitation of Roman models. The face shows no trace of the idealized individualism of the statues of Roman emperors contemporary with it—it remains a mask. The bulging eyes, especially, deny any intention of creating a natural likeness. So stubborn a stylistic tradition reflects the limitations of Celtic art—it is neither able nor willing to free the image of man and animal from the rules imposed by schema. The reasons for this are not so much technical—i. e., the artists' inability to work in the classical manner—as psychological. Their vision of the world and its creatures is affected by primitive taboos which stand in the way of a freer naturalistic approach. This probably also accounts for their ornamental bent. Wherever the Romans or the Germanic tribes stamped out independent Celtic communities, Celtic art disappeared at the same time. Only in Ireland did artists manage to keep their fanciful, self-willed style alive down to the Middle Ages, when they influenced religious art on the Continent through Christian missionaries. But the bronze vessel from Myklebostad, like other richly decorated objects brought to Norway by plundering Vikings, could no longer serve as a model for foreign craftsmen. The enamel inlays and masklike treatment of the human face strike us as oddly Prehistoric survivals in an environment long since opened up to new forms and new conceptions of art. These relics remain a lovely echo of an essentially Prehistoric art, such as could survive only on a remote island on the periphery of Europe.

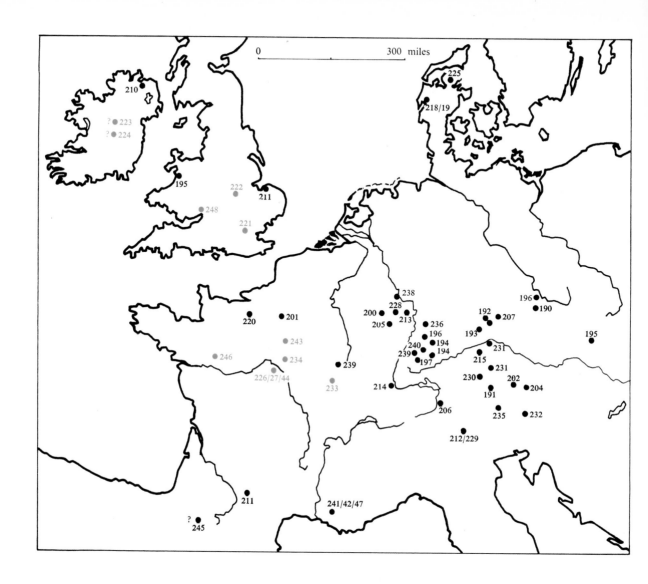

La Tène period sites

Red: Gallo-Roman finds. The find sites of the coins on pp. 216 and 217 are not indicated. To Reinheim (p. 205) belong also pp. 208 and 209. To Kleinaspergle (p. 196) belong also pp. 198, 200 bottom, 202 bottom, and 203.

To some extent, this map resembles that of the Hallstatt sites. Some of the dots represent burials of an aristocratic class, richly furnished with articles of personal adornment, expensive imports, and drinking vessels of the Mediterranean type. But this is true only of certain regions and particularly of those sites dating from the Early La Tène period, and they are therefore not differentiated from the more numerous sites of later date. Finds dating from the Gallo-Roman period stand out more conspicuously as a regional group, testifying to the survival of Celtic art under Roman rule. The emptiness of the Germanic North more or less reflects the actual situation. The sites here contain little that is comparable to Celtic works—the most interesting finds were probably Celtic imports or imitations of Celtic prototypes.

Chronological chart of the La Tène period

The numbers refer to pages. Where the dating is uncertain, a question mark has been added to the page reference.

The La Tène period—so called from a site on Lake Neuchâtel in Switzerland—has been variously subdivided. Here, the system current in South Central Europe has been employed. It is relatively easy to follow the successive stylistic developments, but only the first and the last of these stages can be dated with confidence. This is partly on account of Mediterranean imports—Greek tableware, among other things—which can be fairly reliably dated (cf. p. 198). The final stage (D) is also corroborated by historical records. Stages B and C, however, contain hardly any firmly datable evidence. Essentially, the La Tène period coincides with the rise and decline of the Celtic tribes, the period during which they made their influence felt over large areas of Prehistoric Europe. The warlike expeditions and migrations of the Celts continued into historical times; however, during the first century B.C., their independent states in southern England and on the Continent were destroyed. Caesar subdued Gaul between 58 and 50 B.C. and invaded southern England in 54 B.C. Nevertheless, Celtic styles continued with remarkable persistence. The most brilliant masterpieces of English ornament (see pp. 221 and 222) date from the Roman period. Other regions which, like the kingdom of Noricum, had been under Roman influence for a longer time tended to modify their artistic conception accordingly (see p. 235). In 15 B.C., when the Romans had occupied the Lower Alps as far as the Danube, Celtic traditions lapsed almost completely. In the Germanic North, time limits cannot be so exactly determined, because there is a total lack of historical records and the finds themselves are hard to classify. However, the end of the La Tène epoch is clearly marked by an increase in Roman imports, making a contrast with most of the earlier craftwork which was of Celtic origin (cf. p. 225).

500 B.C.	400	300	200	100	0	100 A.D.

La Tène				Roman Imperial period
A	**B**	**C**	**D**	
	201, 211 bottom, 216, 220, 239 right 241, 242, 245, 247, 252		226, 227? 233, 234 243? 244, 246	GAUL after 58/50, Roman
	195 bottom, 210, 211 top		221–224, 248	BRITISH ISLES after 55/54, partly Roman
			232, 235	NORICUM from 2nd C. on, Roman influence
192, 193 200 bottom 202–205 207–209 228 229 bottom 198 196	191, 194, 195 top, 199 200 top, 213 bottom, 231 236–238, 239 left, 240	197	190, 206 213 top 214, 215 217 229 top 230	CENTRAL EUROPE after 15 B.C., partly Roman Greek import perhaps Greek work
			218, 219 225	SCANDINAVIA Gallic import

251

Openwork ornamental disk. Cast bronze, diameter 2³/₄″, thickness
c. ¹/₂″. From Somme-Bionne (Marne), France. British Museum, London

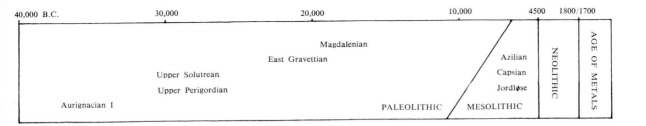

Chronological survey of the Paleolithic era to the La Tène period

Only that portion of the Upper Paleolithic era from which works of art have been preserved is shown. A breakdown of the relatively much shorter Neolithic period and Age of Metals may be found in the charts below and opposite. Of the countless Paleolithic and Mesolithic industries known to us, only those represented in this book are given here. The chronology is relative, any attempt at absolute dating being quite out of the question. For references to illustrations pertinent to any specific industry, see the chronological chart for the Paleolithic and Mesolithic eras on page 51.

4500 B.C.	4000	3500	3000	2500	2000	1700	
						Gumelnitza	SEE
					Stonehenge		WE
CE *Central Europe*					Bell Beaker		CE, WE
NE *Northern Europe*					*Schnurkeramik* (Corded Ware)		CE
WE *Western Europe*					Nordic passage graves		NE
SEE *Southeastern Europe*					Ménec, menhirs		WE
				North German megalithic tombs			CE
				Cucuteni			SEE
				Vadastra			SEE
			Salzmünde				CE
		Moravian painted pottery					CE
		Funnel Beaker					CE, NE
	Wohnplatzkultur (Dwelling Site culture)				*Kammkeramik* (Combed Ware)		NE
Linearbandkeramik (Incised Banded Ware)							CE
LOWER		**MIDDLE**		**UPPER**	**FINAL NEOLITHIC**		

Chronological survey of the Neolithic era

Only those Neolithic industries represented by illustrations in this book are shown. Dates given are approximations, partly arrived at by scientific means. From the third millennium B.C. on, dating is based largely on archaeological comparisons with the advanced historical cultures of the eastern Mediterranean. The various groups were generally divided up into specific zones of Europe. They might, however, like the Bell Beaker and *Schnurkeramik* (Corded Ware) peoples, live side by side in more far-flung regions; or again, like the Vadastra and Salzmünde groups, be the dominant or only culture in a more limited area. For references to the pertinent illustrations, see the chart on page 87.

1800 B.C.	1500	1000	500	0

			Sarmatians	Nomadic horsemen in southeast and Central Europe
		Scythians		
		Early Hallstatt		

BRONZE AGE				URN FIELD PERIOD		HALLSTATT		LA TÈNE				Chronology for Central Europe and peripheral areas
A	B	C	D	A	B	C	D	A	B	C	D	

Mycenae
Early Maltese culture

Nuraghic culture

Phoenicians

Gades (Cádiz)

Carthage

Carthaginians

Greek colonies

Romans

Iberian Celts

Malta
Sardinia

Iberian Peninsula

Mediterranean (east) / (west)

Chronological survey of the Age of Metals

Only peoples and cultures dealt with directly or indirectly in this book are included here. The basic chronology shown is that of Central Europe and its peripheral areas, which, like northern, eastern, and much of western Europe, did not yet have a written history. Events and names of peoples, particularly of the Celtic tribes, are known with any certainty only for the later periods. The first positive dates occur in the Mediterranean area when Aegean states such as Mycenae offer, on account of their trading connections with Crete and Egypt, a relatively early and precise chronology. The western islands such as Malta and Sardinia long retained Prehistoric features. The Iberian Peninsula, on the other hand, joined the ancient peripheral regions as early as the twelfth century B.C., due partially to the founding of Gades (Cádiz) as a Phoenician maritime trading station. The founding of Carthage in 814 B.C. provides an established date for the western Mediterranean area. The Greek colonies along the Iberian coast add to the historical evidence, but darkness still shrouds events in the Celtic Iberian regions. The vicissitudes of the kingdom of Tartessos are similarly obscure. The Carthaginians extended their sphere of influence from the seventh century B.C. on, and in the third century, the Greek colonies lost their independence. In 201 B.C., however, the Second Punic War brought about the downfall of Carthage and of her dominion, and the Iberian Peninsula fell entirely into Roman hands. In 58 B.C., Caesar began the annexation of Gaul and southern Britain to the Roman Empire. On the margins of the historical world, the nomadic peoples of southeastern Europe were continuously astir. For references to the illustrations pertinent to the various groups and periods, see the charts on pages 157, 175, 189, and 251.

Bibliography

GENERAL WORKS OR WORKS DEALING WITH SEVERAL PERIODS

ARMSTRONG, E. C. R., *Guide to the Collection of Irish Antiquities. Catalogue of Irish Gold Ornaments in the Collection of the Royal Irish Academy*, Dublin, 1920

BEHRENS, H., *Archäologische Kostbarkeiten im Landesmuseum für Vorgeschichte Halle an der Saale*, Halle an der Saale, 1958

BRØNDSTED, J., *Danmarks Oldtid*, Gyldendal, 1957–60, 3 vols. German translation: *Nordische Vorzeit*, Neumünster, 1960–63, 3 vols.

FOX, A., *South West England*, New York, 1964

GIOT, P.-R., *Brittany*, New York, 1960

HOERNES, M., *Urgeschichte der bildenden Kunst in Europa von den Anfängen bis um 500 vor Christi*, revised and enlarged by O. Menghin, Vienna, 1925

JAŻDŻEWSKI, K., *Poland*, New York, 1965

KIMMIG, W., and HELL, H., *Vorzeit an Rhein und Donau*, Lindau-Constance, 1958

KLINDT-JENSEN, O., *Denmark before the Vikings*, New York, 1957

KÜHN, H., *Die Kunst Alteuropas*, Stuttgart, 1954

KÜHN, H., *Die vorgeschichtliche Kunst Deutschlands*, Berlin, 1935

LUKAN, K., *Alpenwanderungen in die Vorzeit*, Vienna-Munich, 1965

MANSUELLI, G. A., and SCARANI, R., *L'Emilia prima dei Romani*, Milan, 1961

NEUSTUPNÝ, J., and NEUSTUPNÝ, E., *Czechoslovakia before the Slavs*, New York, 1961

PIDAL, R. M., ed., *Historia de España*, Pt. I, Madrid, 1947–54, 3 vols.

PIGGOTT, S., ed., *The Dawn of Civilization*, New York, 1961

POULÍK, J., and FORMAN, B., *Prehistoric Art* [of Czechoslovakia], Prague-London, 1956

SANDARS, N. K., *Prehistoric Art in Europe*, Baltimore, 1968

SCHELTEMA, F. A. VAN, *Die Kunst des Abendlandes*, Vol. I: *Die Kunst der Vorzeit*, Stuttgart, 1950

STONE, J. F. S., *Wessex before the Celts*, New York, 1958

PALEOLITHIC AND MESOLITHIC

BANDI, H.-G., and MARINGER, J., *Kunst der Eiszeit. Levante Kunst. Arktische Kunst*, Basel, 1952

BANDI, H.-G., et al., *The Art of the Stone Age*, New York, 1961

BATAILLE, G., *Lascaux, or the Birth of Art*, Cleveland, Ohio, 1955

GRAZIOSI, P., *Paleolithic Art*, New York, 1960

LEROI-GOURHAN, A., *Treasures of Prehistoric Art*, New York, 1967

MÜLLER-KARPE, H., *Handbuch der Vorgeschichte*, Vol. I: *Altsteinzeit*, Munich, 1966

NEOLITHIC

BANDI, H.-G., et al., *The Art of the Stone Age*, New York, 1961

DANIEL, G., *The Prehistoric Chamber Tombs of France*, London, 1960

GIOT, P.-R., et al., *Menhirs et dolmens. Monuments mégalithiques de Bretagne*, Châteaulin, 1957 and 1959

HAWKINS, G. S., and WHITE, J. B., *Stonehenge Decoded*, New York, 1965. See also criticism by J. Hawkes, "God in the Machine," in *Antiquity*, 41, 1967, pp. 174ff.

KIRCHNER, H., *Studien aus Alteuropa*, Pt. I: *Eine steinzeitliche "Nerthus"-Darstellung. Zur Innenverzierung der Steinkammer von Züschen* (Festschrift for K. Tackenberg), Cologne, 1964

LE ROUZIC, Z., *Les Monuments mégalithiques de Carnac et de Locmariaquer, leur destination, leur âge*, Carnac, 1953

SCHOPPA, H., "Ein kleinasiatisches Idol aus dem Regierungsbezirk Wiesbaden," in *Ber. ü. d. 5. Intern. Kongr. f. Vor- u. Frühgesch.*, Hamburg, 1958; Berlin, 1961, pp. 734f.

SIMONSEN, P., *Arktiske Helleristninger i Nord-Norge 2*. Oslo, 1958

SPROCKHOFF, E., *Handbuch der Urgeschichte Deutschlands*, Vol. 3: *Die nordische Megalithkultur*, Berlin-Leipzig, 1938

BRONZE AGE TO EARLY IRON AGE

ALTHIN, C.-A., *Studien zu den bronzezeitlichen Felszeichnungen von Skåne*, Lund, 1945

COLES, J. M., "A Rock Carving from South-West Ireland," in *Proceedings of the Prehistorical Society*, 31, 1965, pp. 374f.

DUMITRESCU, V., *Necropola de incinerație din epocha bronzului de la Cîrna*, Bucharest, 1961

GRINSELL, L. V., "The Kivik Cairn, Scania," in *Antiquity*, 16, 1942, pp. 160ff.

HALBERT, H., "Djurskulpturer och Järn från yngre Bronsalder," in *Fornvännen*, 51, 1956, pp. 80ff.

ISSEL, A., *Atti della Società Ligure di Storia Patria*, Vol. 40: *Liguria Preistorica*, Genoa, 1908

JACOB-FRIESEN, K. H., "Die Goldscheibe von Moordorf bei Aurich mit ihren britischen und nordischen Parallelen," in *Jahrb. f. prähist. u. ethnogr. Kunst*, 1931, pp. 25 ff. *Jahresber. d. Hist. Mus. Bern*, 1907, pp. 29 ff.; 1939, p. 98

JOFFROY, R., *Le Trésor de Vix*, Paris, 1954

KASTELIC, J., *Situla Art: Ceremonial Bronzes of Ancient Europe*, New York, 1965

KOSSACK, G., *Römisch-Germanische Forschungen*, Vol. 20: *Studien zum Symbolgut der Urnenfelder- und Hallstattzeit*, Berlin, 1954

KROMER, K., *Das Gräberfeld von Hallstatt*, Florence, 1959

LINDQVIST, S., "The Boat Models from Roos Carr," in *Acta Archaeologica*, 13, 1942, pp. 235 ff.

MONTELIUS, O., *La Civilisation primitive en Italie*, Vol. I, Stockholm, 1895

USLAR, R. VON, "Der Goldbecher von Fritzdorf bei Bonn," in *Germania*, 33, 1955, pp. 321 ff.

ZÜRN, H., "Eine hallstattzeitliche Stele von Hirschlanden, Kr. Leonberg (Württbg.)," in *Germania*, 42, 1964, pp. 27 ff.

WESTERN MEDITERRANEAN

ARRIBAS, A., *The Iberians*, New York, 1964

BREA, L. B., *Sicily before the Greeks*, rev. ed., New York, 1966

EVANS, J. D., *Malta*, New York, 1959

GUIDO, M., *Sardinia*, New York, 1964

HARDEN, D., *The Phoenicians*, New York, 1962

WOODHEAD, A. G., *The Greeks in the West*, New York, 1962

EARLY NOMADIC HORSEMEN

GALLUS, S., and HORVÁTH, T., "Un Peuple cavalier préscythique en Hongrie," in *Dissertationes Pannonicae*, Ser. 2, 9, Budapest, 1939

JETTMAR, K., *Art of the Steppes*, New York, 1967

TALBOT RICE, T., *The Scythians*, New York, 1957

LA TÈNE

BARB, A. A., "Zur Deutung des Kahnfahrers vom Magdalensberg," in *Carinthia*, I, 147, 1957, pp. 90 ff.

DRIEHAUS, J., "Eine frühlatènezeitliche Reiterdarstellung aus Kärlich," in *Bonner Jahrbuch*, 165, 1965, pp. 57 ff.

DUVAL, P.-M., "Les Barques gallo-romaines en bronze de Blessey (Côte-d'Or) et de Cerveau (Saône-et-Loire)," in *Revue Archéologique de l'Est et du Centre-Est*, 3, 1952, pp. 233 ff.

EGGERS, H. J., et al., *Kelten und Germanen in heidnischer Zeit*, Baden-Baden, 1964

FOX, C., *Pattern and Purpose: A Survey of Celtic Art in Britain*, Cardiff, 1958

HENRY, F., *Irish Art in the Early Christian Period*, Ithaca, N. Y., 1965

JACOBSTHAL, P., *Early Celtic Art*, Oxford, 1944, 2 vols.

KELLER, J., *Das keltische Fürstengrab von Reinheim*, Vol. I: *Ausgrabungsbericht und Katalog der Funde*, Mainz, 1965

KLINDT-JENSEN, O., "Archaische Stilzüge in der Spätlatènezeit," in *Ber. ü. d. 5. Intern. Kongr. f. Vor- u. Frühgesch.*, Hamburg, 1958; Berlin, 1961

KLINDT-JENSEN, O., "The Gundestrup Bowl: A Reassessment," in *Antiquity*, 33, 1959, pp. 161 ff.

KRÄMER, W., "Der keltische Bronzetier von Weltenburg in Niederbayern," in *Germania*, 28, 1944–50, pp. 210 ff.

KRÄMER, W., ed., *Neue Ausgrabungen in Deutschland*; article by W. Krämer, *Manching: Ein vindelikisches Oppidum an der Donau*, Berlin, 1958, pp. 175 ff.

Later Prehistoric Antiquities of the British Isles, catalogue of the British Museum, London, 1953

MAIER, F., "Zur bemalten Spätlatènekeramik in Mitteleuropa," in *Germania*, 41, 1963, pp. 259 ff.

MOREAU, J., *Die Welt der Kelten*, Stuttgart, 1958

NOLL, R., *Kunst der Römerzeit in Österreich*, Salzburg, 1949

POBÉ, M., *Art of Roman Gaul*, Toronto, 1961

POWELL, T. G. E., *The Celts*, New York, 1958

SAVORY, H. N., "The Tal-y-Llyn Hoard," in *Antiquity*, 38, 1964, pp. 18 ff.

SCHEFOLD, K., "Stilgeschichte der frühen keltischen Kunst," in *Prähistorische Zeitschrift*, 34/35, 1949/50, Pt. 2, pp. 11 ff.

SCHWARZ, K., "Spätkeltische Viereckschanzen. Ergebnisse der topographischen Vermessung und der Ausgrabungen 1957 bis 1959," in *Jahresber. d. bayer. Bodendenkmalpflege*, 1, 1960, pp. 7 ff.

SCHWARZ, K., "Zum Stand der Ausgrabungen in der spätkeltischen Viereckschanze von Holzhausen," in *Jahresber. d. bayer. Bodendenkmalpflege*, 3, 1962, pp. 22 ff.

Index